Growing A Grateful, Generous Heart

Stewardship Resources

for Children and Their Families

Parent/Family Resource

Living the Good News
a division of The Morehouse Group
600 Grant Street, Suite 400
Denver, CO 80203
1-800-824-1813
www.livingthegoodnews.com

Illustrators: Anne Kosel, Ansgar Holmberg
Cover Design: Nicole Brinn
Writer: Dirk deVries

Living the Good News
    a division of The Morehouse Group
600 Grant Street, Suite 400
Denver, CO 80203

The scripture quotations used herein are from the *Today's English Version Bible—Second Edition.* © 1992 by the American Bible Society. Used by permission.

ISBN 1-931960-16-X

Table of Contents

~~~~~~~~~~~~~~~~~~

Acknowledgements

Special thanks to the following people, all of whom contributed to the creation of these resources. Thank you for your *Grateful, Generous Hearts!*

Terry Parsons

Michael Burke

Dirk deVries

Jim Wahler

Liz Riggleman

Dina Gluckstern

Susan Meaney

Mark Raffinan

Sue MacStravic

Julie Barrett

James Creasey

Ken Quigley

Lisa Hadeen

Steve Mueller

Kathy Coffey

Foreword by Terry Parsons

Missioner for Stewardship and Discipleship,
Episcopal Church Center

The Navajo have a ceremonial for babies known as the First Laugh ceremony. It takes place at an age of several months, when the newborn's gassy smiles have grown into real responses to the people around them, finally erupting into that wonderfully burbling, fist-waving baby-laughter that sounds like no other. When a baby approaches this age and laughter seems imminent, people in the village try to avoid being the one who first makes the baby laugh. The one who prompts that first laughter is the one who provides the meal for the First Laugh ceremony and feeds everyone!

The central activity of the ceremony is feeding the crowd. The baby sits on the lap of the one who caused the laughter. Guests line up and, one by one, baby and host puts food on each plate. The point? To assure that the child grows up to be generous. Later in life, if a child is behaving in a stingy way, it is common for someone to ask whether the child had a First Laugh ceremony.

There are several wonderful assumptions here:
- There is a direct relationship between laughter and generosity. In other words, generosity is fun!
- Generosity can be encouraged, nurtured and taught.
- Encouraging, nurturing and teaching generosity is a community responsibility.
- Generosity is an occasion for community celebration.

We do not have a First Gift ceremony in our church, but perhaps we should. What form might this take in *your* congregation? A brightly colored first offering envelope dropped into the offering plate? A full-fledged ritual complete with special prayers, songs and a procession to the altar to present the first gift? And what might a family ritual look like? Whether family or community ritual, surely it would include a party with all the trimmings.

In our intensely individualistic culture, building a life around the notion that all that we are and all that we have are gifts from God is about as counter-cultural as you can get. We are the people of the "self-made" millionaire, "self-taught" genius and "by-our-own-bootstraps" legends. Yet, teaching that notion that "everything is a gift from you, [God]" (I Chronicles 29:14) is a central theme of Christian theology and a primary focus of this study.

Almost all Christian formation takes place in the home. This makes *you* your children's primary teacher and role model. The good news is that, as you shape your own relationship with God, you have opportunities to help your child do the same.

One of the delights of parenting is helping our children discover their own giftedness, seeing themselves as persons to whom God has given a unique assortment of gifts. An even greater joy is encouraging their discernment of the ways that God hopes they will use these gifts. Of course, in the process of guiding our children, we have the hope of discerning not only our shortcomings and humanness, but some rather wonderful gifts of our own as well.

We are all capable of great generosity. However, it is easy to see the generosity of young children as naive and impractical. What if our childhood generosity—the impulse to give abundantly and outrageously to those we love—is our *true* generosity? Part of this study is about reclaiming the early, fearless generosity that exists before the world imprisons it in the belief that living means overcoming scarcity and distrusting our innate impulse to give. Heaven forbid we ever run out of whatever it is we are about to give away!

May our hearts and those of our children grow in gratitude to God and generosity to God's people all the days of our lives.

A Word about Offerings

The Sunday offering in worship or Sunday School is an essential element in learning how to give. It is a tangible act using something that is a very ordinary piece of everyday life, namely money. It also plays a significant role in developing a sense of abundance.

Please be sure your children have an opportunity to participate in the Sunday offering. If they do not have an allowance, give them an appropriate sum for the church offering. When allowances are introduced, explain that a percentage is to be returned to God. This is the time to talk about tithing, returning one tenth to God. If they attend Children's Church and are not present during the offering in the worship service, make sure an offering is part of the Children's Church or Sunday School. Insist that your congregation honor every giver, making offering envelopes and regular statements available to children as well as adults. I have listened to church treasurers complain about the cost of doing these things. Help them to understand that sending statements to school children are critical investments in the future.

Adult stories of generosity often begin "When I was a child" and involve Sunday School teachers, parents and older relatives who put nickels, dimes or even dollars in small hands and explained that this is one way of telling God "Thank you!" for all that God gives us. The Sunday offering may be your opportunity to play a role in some future philanthropist's story of generosity. More importantly, you may help a child believe not only that God cares for them, but that they have a role in the coming of God's kingdom and the doing of God's will, on earth as it is in heaven.

Chapter 1   How to Use This Book

It's a sticky subject, stewardship. Many of us can remember (but may like to forget!) a way-too-long and far-too-pressured appeal for money, one that left us feeling guilty, anxious and brow-beaten. Do we have to go through this again? We give each week; can't we skip the high-pressure sales pitch? Is this the homily...or a television infomercial?

Well, it's definitely *not* stewardship. It's definitely not what God intended when God made us "stewards" of the vast, inventive, colorful world God created. Stewardship is so much more than fund-raising, so much more than meeting financial goals or giving the national church its due.

In fact, it's so much more, that it might be better to set aside the term *stewardship* for a moment and to start again.

How To Use This Book

So...how *do* you use this book? *You use this book as a resource for helping you and your family deepen your gratitude and increase your generosity.* Hence the title: *Growing a Grateful, Generous Heart.*

If you let it, this book–along with the sessions offered for your children at church–can:
- open your eyes to God's great generosity and love
- encourage you and your family to have a healthy appreciation for all of God's good gifts
- provide simple, fun and practical ways to explore and experience God's generosity and love with your family
- discover and articulate your own attitudes, thoughts, values and feelings about money (as well as time and talent), and consider how to communicate these values to your family
- develop family customs and traditions that reflect gratitude and generosity, connecting with each other, your congregation, your community and the world
- suggest additional ways to explore the basics of stewardship in the weeks and months ahead (and, for that matter, throughout your life and the life of your children)

Getting Started

To begin, read through the first three chapters of this book, which include this introductory chapter and Chapters 2 and 3. This material is for parents only.

In Chapter 2 you'll be given a brief overview of "stewardship." You'll discover what stewardship is, what God intended when God made us all stewards, how stewardship brings us together in Christian community, and what we mean in the Church by such terms as *mission, offering* and *tithing.*

In Chapter 3 you'll find helpful tools for exploring stewardship with your family. Here we address questions like:

- How can I get a handle on my *own* attitudes about stewardship?
- What can our family do to foster healthy habits when it comes to sharing our money, time and talents?

The Next Step

Family involvement starts in Chapter 4. Each of the four sections in Chapter 4 corresponds directly to one of the four sessions your child will experience at church. These sections offer a variety of creative, enjoyable ways for your family to engage together in discovering God's generosity and in learning to share God's gifts with others.

In each of the four sections you will find:

- a brief recap of the scripture story (along with the scripture reference for the story, in case you'd like to read it from the Bible yourself or with your family)
- background on the scripture and a brief reflection (which you can use for your own meditation and/or share with older children and teens)
- a variety of family activities
- suggestions for exploring an additional scripture story that expands the session's theme

The family activities form the heart of this book. We offer lots of options, and we encourage you to pick and choose which ones fit your family. Some activities take only a few minutes; others are more involved. Some are better for older children (grades 3-6 and above), others for younger children (preschool through grade 2), and others for all ages together. Some you can do around the kitchen table while gathered for dinner; others will require collecting materials and spreading out on the living-room floor. Some are weekend or evening outings. We suggest that you read through a session completely, marking those activities that sound most appealing and meaningful.

We've also made the directions crystal clear so each activity will go smoothly. Please don't worry much about "doing it right." The fact that you're taking time to do these activities with your family already says to your children: "God loves you, and I love you too." That message is as important as the point of any activity. And, in fact, that message IS, ultimately, the point of many—maybe all—of the activities!

In fact, that is the point of *Growing a Grateful, Generous Heart*: God loves us, completely and without limits.

And stewardship is, in a nutshell, our response to that love.

But that brings us to Chapter 2.

Chapter 2 Stewardship 101 (An Overview)

What Is Stewardship?

Stewardship is using the gifts God has given us in ways that help us to live the life God calls us to live.

This is the definition we used as we developed the resource you're now reading. Let's break it down and examine it more closely.

Stewardship Is Using the Gifts God Has Given Us...

This God we love and follow—the God of scripture, the God of Christian faith—is a loving, generous God. We have built *Growing a Grateful, Generous Heart* on this foundation of God's love and generosity. It's also the theme of Session 1. From this grounding in God's love and generosity flows our understanding of how God relates to us, how we relate to God, and how we relate to one another.

Our sessions include the story of creation, and we watch in awe as God brings forth a universe of originality, color, beauty, power and surprises. We listen as God pauses repeatedly to say, "Ah, yes...this is very good." We ponder what it means that we, too, are part of God's creative plan, also "very good"...the one part of creation created *in God's image*, of all creatures the ones that "walk and talk with God in the cool of the day," in intimate relationship with God.

The implications are staggering: God wanted to be in communion with us, enough to create us, God's breath becoming ours, God's life force awakening us.

And all of creation ours to celebrate.

It is all *gift*.

Think of all the blessings in your life: God loves you, for starters, and lives with you in intimacy. As much as God loves you, God also cares for you.

And God surrounds you with people who also love and care for you. God gives you family members, friends, coworkers and neighbors to help meet your needs and give your life meaning.

God gives you an amazing body to use as you enjoy God's diverse world. And God gives you enough to eat, a place to live, ways to get about, and activities to make your life rich and meaningful.

It is all *gift*.

...In Ways That Help Us to Live the Life God Calls Us to Live

God asks two things in response to the gift: First, be grateful. Implicit in the "gifting" is the expectation of gratefulness. We don't *earn* gifts; they are given to us. In a sense, they are on loan from God. We don't own them; they are ours to use. That's a reason for gratitude. Live each day with a heart that delights in all you've been given. Don't be critical, whiny, negative. Be grateful. Make a habit of saying, "Thanks, God!"

Second, God asks us to use the gifts responsibly, wisely. Acknowledge them. Celebrate them. Take good care of what you've been given. Preserve, protect and nurture. Share. Be open-hearted with others. Help those with less. Spread the gift around.

Originally, a steward was an employee in a large home or estate, responsible for managing domestic concerns, like servants, upkeep and finances. The steward did not *own* the estate, but had the significant responsibility of maintaining and preserving the owner's property. The concept fits for stewardship in the church today: God says, "Here's my big, beautiful world. Here's your part of it to care for. Here's the land, the home, the people for which I want you to care. Enjoy it all, but care for it well." That's our calling, our mission, to use what God gives us to shape the world the way God wants it.

Growing a Grateful, Generous Heart provides tools to help with both of these tasks, learning greater gratitude and using the gift wisely.

What is Offering?

Each week when we attend worship, someone takes up a collection, an offering. What's that about? It may be so much a part of the Sunday-morning routine that we've never questioned it. That's what they use to pay the utility bills and the salaries, right? Well, yes, but there's more to it than that.

The term *offering* has been around a long time. Put most simply, an offering is *what we freely bring to God*. Offering fits in with our wise use of gifts, part of our calling as stewards.

In the Old Testament, the people of Israel gave, not just any old part of the harvest, flock or herd, but the "first-fruits," the first and best of what they had grown or raised. The offering wasn't an afterthought, but a *first*-thought: God has given us this bounty. Before we enjoy it, let's say thanks by giving back the best to God!

If it isn't of value to us, it isn't an offering. Recall the two copper coins given by the poor widow (the story we explore in Session 3): Jesus identifies her small offering as a *huge* offering, because what she gave was *huge* to her—it was all she had! *All she had!* Imagine emptying your cupboards, closets and drawers, your bank account, your stock portfolios...and bringing them all to church next Sunday. The widow's offering humbles us with the depth of sacrifice it represents.

Offering requires faith. It's a physical expression of our faith, because it operates on the assumption that what I need, God will provide.

What Is Tithing?

The custom of tithing, giving 10% of your money and/or possessions to a king or deity, comes to us from ancient times. In the Bible, we first hear of it in Genesis 14, when Abraham gives the priest-king Melchizedek a tenth of his loot after returning from battle. The first mention of tithing to God is the promise Jacob makes in Genesis 28:22 when he says to God, "...and I will give a tenth of everything you give me." Various Old Testament regulations also call for tithing...of fruits and grains, of livestock, of wine and oil, even of honey. The Levities (the priests) were to live on a tithe of the tithe.

But tithing is less prominent in the New Testament. Several references assume its continued existence, but nowhere are we enjoined to tithe as were the Israelites in the Old Testament. Jesus' only reference to tithing comes as a criticism of the teachers and the Pharisees, who are scrupulous about tithing their spices, but "neglect to obey the really important teachings of the Law" (Matthew 23:23). Jesus does not condemn tithing but the legalism that ignored its purpose. The essence of tithing is a grateful acknowledgement of God as the generous source of all that we possess. On a practical level it becomes the means by which we care for the poor and strive for justice.

Tithing is, in fact, a part of Episcopal polity. Beginning in 1983 and at each subsequent General Convention, deputies have approved resolutions affirming the tithe as "the minimum standard of giving." A helpful way to think about tithing is from the perspective of "first fruits." The "firstness" of the tithe is a better place to begin than its "tenthness." In other words, adopt the concept of giving a percentage of the family's resources to God—whatever seems appropriate to your unique family situation—but make that gift the first expenditure each week or month.

Stewards in Community

We live, learn, grow, work and worship in community. God creates us for and shapes us within community—family, neighborhood, congregation, town or city, and beyond. What are the implications for stewardship? Stewards are formed in community. Our children, right now, whether we realize it or not, whether we intend it or not, are being molded into stewards. What kind of stewards are our children becoming?

If we model acquiring, hoarding, consuming and wasting, we create stewards who acquire, hoard, consume and waste. These kinds of stewards would have lost their estate jobs quickly.

When we model giving, conserving, sharing and simple living, we create stewards who give, conserve, share and live simply. It sounds obvious, but it's critical. These kinds of stewards are responsible and valuable to the health and survival of not only their families and congregations, but ultimately of the rest of God's creation as well. And, as a happy by-product, they live closer to God, with more joy and greater faith.

Stewardship is taught, or perhaps more accurately, *caught*, in community—in congregations like yours (which is why your church has adopted this program, *Growing a Grateful, Generous Heart*) and in families like yours (which is why you're reading these words in the first place!). The steward is a servant of the household, the community.

Not only do we *catch* stewardship in community, we *practice* it in community as well. The community, whether your family, your circle of friends, your congregation or the world, provides the opportunities to practice sharing God's gifts. The Sunday offering mentioned earlier is one such opportunity: "Here, take this," we say, "and use it to pay for the heat and the phone. And give some of it for relief efforts and some to help run the national church." Our values are reflected through our practice. How does your family decide what to give and to whom? What projects do you take on to help the needy? to curb your "consumer appetites"? to recognize when "enough is enough"? (We'll give you concrete, manageable suggestions later in this book.) If there's ever an area where it's important to practice what you preach, it's stewardship. It all falls flat when not backed up by simple practice.

Stewardship: Modeled in community. Practiced in community. You and your family are the community, not the *entire* community, but the most fundamental and foundational part of the community.

In Chapter 3, we explore more of what that means for you and your children.

Chapter 2: Stewardship 101 (An Overview)

Chapter 3 Stewardship, Children and Families

Children and Gratitude

Children are naturally grateful. We see it in the way they delight in a passing fire truck, a bit of shared silliness or a crunchy carpet of autumn leaves. To foster such moments, offer time and opportunity for children to enter fully into the world around them, whether the natural world outside our homes, or the safe spaces we create within.

In Chapter 4 we suggest practical ways to open up such time and space for your family. In general, though, it requires a deepened awareness of our immediate surroundings as a constant revelation of God's generosity. God *is* generous, whether we realize it or not. Cultivating the awareness means pausing, letting go, for at least a few minutes, of the pressure and hassle that consume us, listening, looking, being quiet. What, in this moment, is good? As I look around me, what do I see that is beautiful, interesting, a gift from God? What can I hear? What am I able to do, right now, that I usually take for granted. Can I see, walk, laugh, hug, call a friend, have a snack? As we will see in the next few weeks, all is gift. Take time each day to be quiet enough to remember this.

Then, do that with your family. Make a habit of allowing space to look around, to listen, to breathe slowly and deeply, to be aware of the simple, real and meaningful blessings in your family's life. It can be as simple as a mealtime ritual during which you ask, "What is good for you, right at this moment? What would you like to thank God for right now?"

Children also learn gratitude through modeling. Grateful parents tend to raise grateful kids. As parents, do we rejoice in a refreshing, life-giving spring rain, or do we complain of the inconvenience of boots and umbrellas? Do we say thanks when our child helps set the table, or do we point out that the fork is on the wrong side of the plate? Are we aware of the blessings God pours into our lives each day, or are we focused on what we still imagine we lack, what others have that we don't or what else we "deserve"? It may be a cliche, but the implications of the old saying are significant: Is my glass half empty or half full?

Not only is gratitude an appropriate response to God's generosity, it's also a healthy life skill. If *we* develop it, so will our kids, and we will all be more productive, happier, connected children of God... the way God meant us to be.

Children and Generosity

In *Growing a Grateful, Generous Heart* we suggest that a natural consequence of our gratitude for God's good gifts will be generosity, the willingness to share with others.

It's important not to impose adult expectations of generosity on children—particularly expectations that most adults don't meet themselves. So before we start planning how the children in our lives ought to give, we can start by examining our own corporate and individual behaviors around stewardship. For example, to what extent do our friends, family members and neighbors experience our generosity? Are we known for loaning tools? sharing meals? praising the accomplishments of others? watching the neighbors' kids? giving to local charities? contributing baked goods for church meetings? listening when someone needs to vent? donating clothes and household items we no longer need? Just as with gratitude, *we cannot teach what we do not model.*

it is also important to respect the normal developmental stages of children. Behavior that would be selfish in a mature adult may be an important part of a child's normal growth. For example, children cannot give what they have never owned. Be cautious about forcing a young child to share his or her toys with other children. We may be tempted to use our size and authority to make a child share, without realizing that the child has yet to experience or understand ownership.

This does not mean, however, that there are no appropriate ways to share stewardship values with young children. It is also an ordinary part of young lives to learn to care for things around us. Young children are often especially happy to be invited into our ordinary routines of caretaking: washing dishes, using a feather duster, feeding the family pet or turning a hose on the family car. Here adult leadership is crucial: do we ourselves see these simple activities as opportunities to show grateful care for the good things in our lives? This generous spirit is well-manifested in the way we handle the objects that grace our lives, treating them with respect, and, at times, even affection. The act of folding laundry offers a good example: Think about that towel. Warm, clean and fresh-smelling, it will soon embrace your wet, squirming, giggling son or daughter...a simple object made sacred by a nearly sacramental moment of affection and caring. Consider this as you finish that final fold and place the towel in the linen closet. Let your children see the joy you take—and your gratitude—for such simple, everyday pleasures.

We foster generosity and empathy in young children primarily through the environment of relationships that we provide. Children who experience consistently that their own sadness, loneliness or anger is met with a generous, compassionate response are best equipped to offer these responses themselves. We cannot substitute for this concrete experience an abstract activity that asks them to collect money for people they will never see, suffering they will never share. An activity in which children regularly meet with an adopted grandparent who needs small amounts of help, for example, is more valuable to children than a onetime drive to collect money for the hungry overseas. An inventory of your family's face-to-face ministries will turn up the most fruitful opportunities for family outreach activities.

Other Resources for Families

The resources listed below are a sampling of what you might find at a bookstore, online or at your local library. Some address the desire to live a simpler, more earth- and people-friendly lifestyle. Some deal directly with money issues and how to communicate about money with your children. Still others offer ways to explore and appreciate God's creation.

In addition to the resources listed here, you'll find additional suggestions in the sessions in Chapter 4.

Books for Parents

Andrews, Cecile. *The Circle of Simplicity*. New York: HarperCollins, 1997.

Clapp, Rodney, ed. *The Consuming Passion*. Downer's Grove, IL: InterVarsity Press, 1998.

Cornell, Joseph. *Sharing Nature with Children*. Nevada City, CA: Dawn Publications, 1998.

_____ . *Sharing Nature with Children II*. Nevada City, CA: Dawn Publications, 1999.

DeWitt, Calvin. *Earth-Wise*. Kalamazoo, MI: CRC Publications, 1994.

Dominquez, Joe and Vicki Robin. *Your Money or Your Life: Transforming Your Relationship with Money and Achieving Financial Independence*. New York: Penguin, 1999.

Duensing, Edward. *Talking to Fireflies, Shrinking the Moon: Nature Activities for All Ages*. Golden, CO: Fulcrum, 1997.

Dungan, Nathan. *Prodigal Sons & Material Girls: How Not to be Your Child's ATM*. New York: John Wiley & Sons, 2003.

Elgin, Duane. *Voluntary Simplicity: Toward a Way of Life That Is Outwardly Simple, Inwardly Rich*. New York: Quill, 1993.

Glickman, Marshall. *The Mindful Money Guide: Creating Harmony Between Your Values and Your Finances*. New York: Ballantine Wellspring, 1999.

Good Times Made Simple: The Lost Art of Fun. Takoma Park, MD: The Center for a New American Dream.

Levering, Frank and Wanda Urbanska. *Simple Living: One Couple's Search for a Better Life*. New York: Viking, 1992.

Lingelbach, Jenepher and Lisa Purcell, eds. *Hands-On Nature: Information and Activities for Exploring the Environment with Children*. Lebanon, NH: University Press of New England, 2000.

Lockwood, Georgene. *The Complete Idiot's Guide to Simple Living*. New York: Alpha Books, 2000.

Luhrs, Janey. *The Simple Living Guide: A Sourcebook for Less Stressful, More Joyful Living*. New York: Broadway Books, 1997.

Myers, David. *The Pursuit of Happiness*. New York: Avon Books, 1992.

Owen, David. *The First National Bank of Dad: The Best Way to Teach Kids about Money*. New York: Simon & Schuster, 2003.

Pierce, Linda Breen. *Choosing Simplicity: Real People Finding Peace and Fulfillment in a Complex World*. Carmel, CA: Gallagher Press, 2000.

Ryan, John C., and Alan Thein Durning. *Stuff*. Seattle, WA: Northwest Environment Watch, 1997.

Schut, Michael. *Food and Faith: Justice, Joy and Daily Bread*. Denver, CO: Living the Good News, 2002.

_____ . *Simpler Living, Compassionate Life: A Christian Perspective*. Denver, CO: Living the Good News, 1999.

Sherlock, Marie. *Living Simply with Children: A Voluntary Simplicity*. New York: Three Rivers Press, 2003.

St. James, Elaine. *Simplify Your Life*. New York: Hyperion, 1994.

Taylor, Betsy. *What Kids Really Want That Money Can't Buy*. New York: Warner Books, 2003.

Chapter 3: Stewardship, Children and Families

Books for Kids

Baylor, Byrd. *The Table Where Rich People Sit*. New York: Aladdin, 1998.

Berenstain, Stan and Jan Berenstain. *The Berenstain Bears' Dollars and Sense*. New York: Random House, 2001.

_____ . *The Berenstain Bears' Trouble with Money*. New York: Random House, 1983.

Brown, Marc. *Authur's Pet Business*. Boston, MA: Little, Brown and Company, 1993.

Brumbeau, Jeff. *The Quiltmaker's Gift*. New York: Scholastic, 2001.

Buckley, Ray. *The Give-Away: A Christmas Story*. Nashville, TN: Abingdon Press, 1999.

Chinn, Karen. *Sam and the Lucky Money*. New York: Lee & Low Books, 1997.

Flake, Sharon G. *Money Hungry*. New York: Jump at the Sun, 2001.

Harman, Hollis Page. *Money Sense for Kids*. Hauppauge, NY: Barrons, 1999.

Karlitz, Gail and Debbie Honig. *Growing Money: A Complete Investing Guide for Kids*. New York: Price Stern Slone, 1999.

Leedy, Loreen. *Follow the Money!* New York: Holiday House, 2002.

Mayer, Gina and Mercer Mayer. *Just a Piggy Bank*. New York: Golden Books, 2001.

Mollel, Tololwa. *My Rows and Piles of Coins*. Boston: Clarion Books, 1999.

Viorst, Judith. *Alexander, Who Used to Be Rich Last Sunday*. Glenview, IL: Scott Foresman, 1980.

Wells, Rosemary. *Bunny Money*. London: Puffin, 2000.

Websites

Affluenza: *www.pbs.org/kcts/affluenza*

Center for a New American Dream: *www.newdream.org*

Earth Ministry: *www.earthministry.com*

Episcopal Church Environmental Stewardship Office: *www.episcopalchurch.org/peace-justice/ envstewardship.asp*

Episcopal Relief and Development: *www.er-d.org*

Episcopal Stewardship Office: *www.episcopalchurch.org/congdev/Stewardship/Steward.htm*

Seeds of Simplicity: *www.seedsofsimplicity.org*

United Thank Offering: *www.episcopalchurch.org/uto*

Chapter 4 Activities for Your Family

Overview

We've divided Chapter 4 into four sessions, paralleling the four sessions of the *Growing a Grateful, Generous Heart* stewardship program. Each has two parts:

■ *Part One: For Parents* offers material just for you, the parent. Here you'll find a summary of the session activities, background on the week's scripture and a meditation. Part One is for your personal growth, not for your children. (Although you're free to share this material with older children, if you think it's appropriate.)

■ *Part Two: For Families* provides dozens of options for family activities, all of which support the session theme. Pick as few or as many of these as you'd like to do.

If you take the time now to review these materials, you'll be a step ahead. You can put checkmarks beside activities you'd like to include. (We provide a box before each activity for this.) If you start now to plan for upcoming activities, you'll allow yourself time to gather materials or make special arrangements. Remember: *pick and choose!* We offer many different activities; your job is to select those that fit your family's time and interest.

SESSION 1 The Good Shepherd

Part One: FOR PARENTS

Scripture

John 10:11-18, 27-28

Theme

God loves us without limits.

Objectives

■ to introduce and explore the image of Jesus as the Good Shepherd
■ to understand how much God loves us
■ to encourage trust in God's loving care

Activities

■ Story: The Good Shepherd
■ Checking In
■ Giving Box
■ Stewardship Prayer
■ Art Response
■ Around the Table
■ Field Trip
■ Second Story: More on the Good Shepherd
■ Music
■ Praying Together

Scripture Summary

Jesus uses the image of a caring, self-sacrificing shepherd to describe how intimately he knows us, how deeply he loves us and how far he goes to protect us. Jesus knows each of us by name and promises all of us eternal life.

Chapter 4, Session 1: The Good Shepherd

Scripture Background

This reading portrays Jesus as "the good shepherd." Despite centuries of village and city living, the Jews still held on to the image of the shepherd as an ideal of good governing. But more importantly, this image revealed the kind of character that was required for Christians who assumed responsibility for leadership in the community. We still call our leaders "pastors," which is derived from the Latin word for a shepherd.

In Greek, the word for *good* means beautiful and describes something that is free from defects and thus is praiseworthy, noble and an ideal of perfection. Here it might be better translated as *model*. Jesus is the model shepherd, both because of his faithfulness to those under his care and because of his intimate knowledge of them, which parallels the relationship between the Father and the Son.

In the Old Testament, God is called the Shepherd of Israel (Psalm 23:1, 80:1; Isaiah 40:11; Jeremiah 31:10; Ezekiel 34:11-16) as is David or the Messiah (Psalm 78:70-72; Ezekiel 37:24; Micah 5:4). God's covenant responsibility, like that of the father of a household or the shepherd of a flock, required providing for the needs and protecting from harm all those in the group. God's love or attachment to the members of the community is demonstrated daily through this attention to their needs.

Jesus fulfills the requirements of a good shepherd because he will not flinch at danger—even laying down his life to protect those under his care. Moreover, his intimate knowledge of each individual reveals his particular love for each one. His loving care is always directed to our welfare and his only aim is that we all learn to be his one flock.

As an image of God's boundless love for us, Jesus the Good Shepherd invites us to imitate his example. Since we are known and loved so intimately by Jesus, we are to imitate this love in providing and caring for others. We cannot count the cost or quit when hardships come. Good stewardship is good shepherding—providing for the needs of others and protecting the vulnerable from harm.

Reflection and Response

Imagine a charismatic leader, with the kind of personality people are drawn to and a style that people want to imitate. Imagine, furthermore, that some awful sacrifice is required to keep these followers alive. This brave, attractive person doesn't flinch but steps forward at once, generously offering his or her life in exchange for the people's safety.

The good news is that this imagined leader who may seem too good to be true is in fact Jesus, our shepherd. In this role, he shows us several dimensions relevant to stewardship. As we seek to shepherd our resources as carefully as he shepherds us, four aspects of this dynamic are relevant to our search:

First, Jesus has intimate knowledge of his followers: "I know my sheep and they know me" (vv. 14-15). Parents or church leaders should pay attention. He has suffered with his people and knows what they want. He will not demand what they cannot do or force on them what they do not need.

A second noteworthy element is the lack of coercion exerted by the Shepherd. His voice is all, and it is enough. We often meet with resistance when we try to persuade another; we also witness the remarkable change that inner motivation can produce. Jesus knows well the drawing power of love and the strength of people driven by love.

Another significant factor is that Jesus differentiates himself from the hired man, who abandons the sheep when he sees the wolf coming. Those who understand stewardship best say it's not only about money; it's not even initially about money. It is, instead, about spirituality. It is the heart's quiet answer to a question that may ultimately be unanswerable: "What can I offer the Lord for all his goodness to me?" (Psalm 116:12).

Finally, the essence of stewardship is gratitude. Knowing we have a superb leader who will give his life for us, we want to do all we can for this splendid figure, this Jesus. Gratitude spills over in service to others. It is heartening to know that the original meaning for "good" was "beautiful." Human beings are drawn to beauty as to the fragrance of fresh flowers. Thus, our stewardship is not onerous drudgery, but a perfectly natural, heartfelt response.

If someone tells us, "I give them eternal life, and they shall never die. No one can snatch them away from me," (v. 28) we should feel deeply secure, inordinately thankful. We would also want to give this comfort to the children in our care. As the work of Sofia Cavalletti, author of *The Religious Potential of the Child* has shown, even children who are critically ill respond naturally and immediately to the Good Shepherd. They derive from the parable "a serene peace," knowing that they are called intimately by name and protected. Such a caring figure inspires children—and all of us—to goodness.

Read through the scripture passage. Quietly consider:
■ At this time in my life, what could be my grateful response to the Good Shepherd?

_____

_____

_____

_____

_____

_____

_____

_____

My Own Story

Money Matters
■ Think back to your childhood. What are your earliest memories of money and possessions? Did your family seem to have enough? not enough?
■ What were your parents' values when it came to money and possessions? How were those values communicated? through word? through action?
■ When you finally moved out on your own, to what extent did you take with you your parents' attitudes, feeling and beliefs about money and possessions? If other factors helped shape your early attitudes toward money, what were they?

■ To what extent *now* have your beliefs and values about money and possessions shifted from that of your parents?
■ Over the years, how deliberate or intentional have you been about shaping and expressing an "ethic of money and possessions"? What has that looked like?
■ Complete this statement: "When it comes to money, I believe..."

_____

_____

_____

_____

_____

_____

_____

_____

Consume, Spend, Get
■ Our culture stresses acquisition and ownership, valuing those who have over those who have not. To what extent have you experienced this yourself? In what ways do you think your children also experience this?
■ The average American child watches 55 television commercials *every day*. What impact does advertising have on your family life? on its values? on its behavior?
■ If someone monitored what your family spent in a typical month (on groceries, household items, clothing, entertainment, etc.), what would they list as your family's "Top Ten Values"?

_____

_____

_____

_____

_____

_____

Story: The Good Shepherd

Soon after your child hears the story of the Good Shepherd in the session at church, review the story together, perhaps at the conclusion of a meal or just before bedtime. Children appreciate repetition, so don't hesitate to repeat the story several times, perhaps choosing several different approaches throughout the week.

Story Options

☐ *Child's Storytelling (with or without props)*
Invite your child to tell you the story of the Good Shepherd as he or she recalls it from the week's session at church. If you have a figure of either Jesus or the Good Shepherd, let children retell the story using the figure. Clumps of cotton balls could be used for sheep, and a stuffed animal could stand in for a wolf or a bear. A construction toy (for example, building blocks, Legos or Lincoln Logs) could be used to construct a sheepfold. Invite children into the process of finding and adapting props from around the house. If you have a child's toy farm set, you may also be able to use those figures to tell the story.

☐ *Children's Paper*
Look together at the Children's Paper that your child brought home from his or her session. Grades 1-2 could read the story to the family, perhaps at the conclusion of a meal together. Children in grades 3-6 could read the story directly from the Bible.

☐ *Children's Bible*
Read together the story of the Good Shepherd from a children's Bible or Bible storybook, for example:
— *Tomie dePaola's Book of Bible Stories* by Tomie dePaola (New York: G. P. Putnam's Sons/Zondervan, 1990)

☐ *Children's Books*
Read one of the following books together:
— *Psalm 23* by Tim Ladwig (Grand Rapids, MI: Wm. B. Eerdmans Publishing CO, 1997)
— *Jesus the Good Shepherd* by Robert D. Mitchell (St. Louis, MO: Concordia, 1989)

— *Jesus, the Good Shepherd* by Marilyn Perry (Kenowa, BC: Wood Lake, 2000)

Checking In

Discover what your child *really* thinks and feels about our great, loving God. Here are several activities to help children express themselves. Remember, no matter what responses you might get—even ones that surprise you—affirm all answers, respect your child's feelings and opinions, and occasionally restate what your child says to make sure you've understood.

Check-In Options

☐ *Family Talk—God's Love*
Discuss the following questions, being certain to share your answers as well:
— How much does God love you?
— Why do you think God loves you so much?
— How do you know God loves you?
— In what ways does God care for you? protect you?
— What would you like to say to God about God's love for you?

☐ *Good Shepherd Drawings*
Give each family member a sheet of drawing paper. Spread out a box of crayons or colored felt markers and ask everyone to draw a picture of themselves with Jesus, the Good Shepherd. When finished, ask:
— What's happening in your picture?
— What might the Good Shepherd be saying to you in your drawing?
— What are you saying to the Good Shepherd?

☐ *Write a Prayer*
Using a large sheet of light-colored construction paper and a colored felt marker, together write a prayer to Jesus, our Good Shepherd. You could begin with:
— Dear Jesus, Good Shepherd, ...

Chapter 4, Session 1: The Good Shepherd

Giving Box

The "Giving Box" is a tradition familiar to many Episcopal families. Many parishes use "the blue box" from UTO (United Thank Offering, 1-800-903-5544, *www.episcopalchurch.org/uto*). Together with family members, you can create your own Giving Box using the pattern on page 55. Enlarge the pattern on a photocopier, transfer it onto heavy paper or cardboard, then cut it out and assemble it by matching the letters on the tabs. Decorate the box as you wish, with your own title, construction paper, markers, gift wrap and ribbons, etc. For suggestions on using your Giving Box, see the *Giving Box Options* below.

Note: Your Giving Box could just as easily be a Giving Jar, Giving Can or Giving Basket. Use any available container and, as a family, decorate it using construction paper, markers, ribbon, wrapping paper, assorted trims or other materials.

Giving Box Options

☐ *Giving Box*
As a family, choose an organization or individual to whom you'd like to make a donation. (If you don't have a charity in mind, talk with the people at church who are organizing *Growing a Grateful, Generous Heart*. They will likely have suggestions for you, or possibly a parish-wide project in which you can participate.) Keep the box where your family gathers frequently (kitchen table, TV room, etc.). Make it a habit, at least daily, to talk about the box, including who will receive the money, why you selected this recipient, and how the money might get used. Make putting money into the box a family ritual; as you contribute, talk about where the money is coming from (change from lunch, a portion of an allowance, etc.), and why you want it to go into the Giving Box. You might light a candle as you begin, and conclude with the Stewardship Prayer *(see below)*.

☐ *Blessing Box*
A Giving Box can hold more than money. Consider using your Giving Box as a Blessing Box. Instead of (or in addition to) putting in money, make available slips of paper and a pen or pencil and ask family members to write out "blessings" for each other, for extended family members, for friends and for others around the world whom they believe could use a blessing.

☐ *Thanksgiving Box*
You could also use your Giving or Blessing Box as a place to collect slips of paper on which family members have written things they're grateful for, like a warm new coat, a faithful cat or dog, a loving grandparent or the ability to run fast or jump high. Once a week, perhaps at a Sunday meal together, open the box and review the things for which your family is grateful.

☐ *Everything Box*
If you wish, combine the above ideas, or invent other ways to use your Giving Box.

Stewardship Prayer

In the sessions at church, some children are learning this prayer, repeating it every week at the conclusion of their sessions. You could also use the prayer at home throughout the four weeks of *Growing a Grateful, Generous Heart*. See the *Options* following the prayer.

Prayer:
Thank you, Jesus, for bringing us together in your love.
Thank you for giving us everything we need.
Help us to take good care of the gifts you've given us.
Help us to use them to do your work. *Amen.*

Stewardship Prayer Options

☐ *Prayer Poster*
Together make a prayer poster by copying the Stewardship Prayer onto a large piece of paper or poster board. Decorate the prayer with fabric scraps, colored markers, buttons, etc. Tape or tack the prayer near the dining table or beside your child's bed. Pray it together whenever possible.

☐ *Memory Prayer*
Say one line of the Stewardship Prayer and invite other family members to repeat it back to you.

Chapter 4, Session 1: The Good Shepherd

Depending on the age of your children, you could memorize a new line each day or two, or wait a week before adding the next line.

☐ *Prayer Booklet*
Using drawing paper and crayons, invite each family member to draw a response to a line of the prayer. You might do this for the first line this week (dealing with God's love for us), saving the second line for next week after the children have talked about God's good gifts to us in Session 2 at church. Later, combine these drawings, along with the words of the prayer, into a booklet. Stack pages, punch holes, and tie together with yarn. Or simply punch holes in the pages and keep them together in an inexpensive three-ring binder.

Art Response ⋁⋀⋁⋀⋁⋀⋁⋀

Complete one or more of the art projects suggested below. Remember, the goal is not the final product, but the time spent together exploring the Bible story and learning about each other.

Art Options

☐ *Sheep and Shepherd Mural*
Create a sheep and shepherd mural somewhere in your home. Cut out simple sheep shapes from construction paper and glue cotton balls to them. Label each one with a family member's name. Create additional sheep named for friends and any other people important to the family (teachers, neighbors, etc.). Older children can decorate a large sheet of poster board or strip of newsprint or butcher paper to look like a place of safety and refuge, for example, a pastoral countryside, an urban park or a grandparent's living room. (Let the children decide what the setting should be.) Ask family members to tape or glue their sheep to the mural. (More sheep can be added throughout the week as family members think of other people they'd like to add.) Now talk together about adding Jesus, the Good Shepherd to the mural: Where would he be? What would he be doing? Together add Jesus to the poster.

☐ *Sheep Sock Puppets*
Create sheep sock puppets using clean, discarded socks. To make a puppet, put the sock on your hand and push the heel into your hand to make the mouth. Glue felt eyes above the mouth and a pink or red felt tongue inside the mouth. With family members, act out the story of the Lost Sheep, Luke 15:1-7. Take turns playing *the lost sheep* and *the shepherd*. You could also take turns hiding one of the sock-puppet sheep from the others; everyone else can search until they find the "lost sheep." Talk about how it feels to be lost and then found.

☐ *Sheep Greeting Cards*
Create sheep greeting cards for someone who could benefit from some attention and a reminder that God loves them without limit: Start with sheets of colored construction paper, folded in half. Draw a sheep shape on the front of the card, then fill the shape with glued-on fabric scraps, cotton balls or shredded foam. Inside write a message of encouragement and perhaps a scripture quotation such as "I am the Good Shepherd" (John 10:11) or "I myself will be the shepherd of my sheep, and I will find them a place to rest" (Ezekiel 34:25).

Around the Table ⋁⋀⋁⋀⋁⋀

Family mealtimes, either at home or out, can be a great place to continue exploring the weekly themes of *Growing a Grateful, Generous Heart.*

Discussion Options

☐ *Family Talk–Who Cares for Us?*
Discuss the following questions, being certain to share your answers as well:
— Who is like a shepherd to us? Who takes care of us at home? at school? when playing with friends? when we are sick? when we're feeling lonely, frightened or sad?

Sentence Completions

Finish one or more of these statements:

— Jesus, you're like a shepherd to me when you...
— The best thing about having you as my Good Shepherd, Jesus, is...
— One way in which I can be like a shepherd to someone else is...

Family Talk–Names

Discuss the following questions, being certain to share your answers as well:

— How did you get your name?
— What does your name mean?
— What pet names (nicknames) do you have?
— Why does it feel good when someone remembers our name? calls us by name?

Family Talk–Being Shepherds

Discuss the following questions, being certain to share your answers as well:

— Whom do *we* take care of? For whom are we like shepherds? *(for example, pets, other family members, friends)*
— When in our family do we show God's love to each other?
— In what ways can we bring God's love to other kids at school? to our brothers and sisters? to our grandparents? to people who live nearby? to people who don't have enough to eat or a place to sleep?

Field Trip

Plan to take your family on an outing to experience, explore and share God's love.

Field Trip Options

Family Visit

Spend an evening with another family from your congregation–or from another faith community. Spend an hour or two playing games. Talk about helping each other with some family or household project.

Farm Visit

If you live in a rural area, arrange to visit someone who raises sheep. Pet the sheep and watch them for a while. Help the owner feed and water the sheep. Ask the owner about raising sheep: What are sheep like? What makes raising sheep fun? challenging? What does the owner do for the sheep to keep them safe, clean and healthy?

Donations

Put together a few bags of grocery items, used clothes or used toys and games. Donate them to

Second Story:
More on the Good Shepherd

Especially for older children, it can be challenging and revealing to link scripture stories with similar themes. This week, if you wish, explore additional scriptures dealing with God's role as our loving, caring shepherd.

Scripture Options:
- Psalm 23
- Isaiah 40:10-11
- Ezekiel 34:11-16
- Luke 15:1-7

If you choose to introduce one or more of these alternative scriptures, feel free to adapt any other activity from the session to explore it further (like having children retell the story, acting out the story using sock puppets or illustrating the story with a family mural). Most simply, you could read the story from the Bible with your child, then discuss:

- What more do we learn about God's love for us in this story?
- How do you feel when you hear this story? loved? safe? happy?
- What would you like to say to God, right now?

a local shelter or food bank. While you're there dropping off the items, visit with the people who work there; ask how the things you donate will be distributed and used. Talk to the people who use the service; find out what life is like for them.

☐ *Adopt a Neighbor*
"Adopt" a neighbor or congregation member who has trouble getting around and could use some help each week running errands, cleaning their home or yard, answering mail, etc. As a family, spend an hour or two each week helping this person.

Whatever outing you plan, take time during the trip and after to discuss what happened, how family members are feeling and what they're thinking about.

Music

If your family sings together, learn and enjoy the following song. Note that the four verses of the song correspond to the four sessions of *Growing a Grateful, Generous Heart.* We will refer back to this song in future sessions. This week, learn just the first verse and the chorus.

Friends with God

Words and music by Pamela L. Hughes

3. And God loved the widow
   Who gave up all she had.
   She was a friend of Jesus,
   And that made Jesus glad.

4. Jesus called to Peter,
   "Come on and follow me.
   We'll walk this world together,
   And friends we'll always be!"

Music Option

☐ Write new verses that include the names of family members and friends, for example:

Jesus is Beth's Shepherd,
Who cares and loves her so.
He is Beth's friend forever
No matter where she goes.

Chapter 4, Session 1: The Good Shepherd

Praying Together 〰〰〰

There are as many ways to pray as there are people who pray. Each week we'll suggest a few ideas to choose from.

Prayer Options

☐ *Prayer Book*

From *The Book of Common Prayer*, pray the Collect for the Fourth Sunday of Easter, found on page 225.

☐ *Psalm Prayer*

Pray Psalm 23 from a children's Bible.

☐ *Arrow Prayers*

Offer "arrow prayers": In an arrow prayer, you take turns saying one or two words in response to a prayer topic. You could start with the topic "the Good Shepherd." What words come to mind? "Jesus" "Protection." "Cool water." "Green grass." "Play." What words describe your feelings? "Safe." "Contented." "Loved." "At peace." Close by saying *Amen* together.

☐ *Prayer Song*

Sing the song from today's Session, "Friends with God."

☐ *Stewardship Prayer*

Learn and pray the Stewardship Prayer, found earlier in this session on page 21.

Chapter 4, Session 1: The Good Shepherd

Growing a Grateful, Generous Heart: Parent/Family Resource 〰〰

SESSION 2 Creation

Part One: FOR PARENTS

ᐯᐯᐯᐯᐯᐯᐯᐯᐯᐯᐯᐯᐯᐯᐯᐯᐯᐯᐯᐯᐯᐯᐯᐯᐯᐯᐯᐯᐯᐯᐯᐯᐯᐯᐯ

Scripture
Genesis 1:1–2:4

Theme
Everything we have is a gift from God.

Objectives
- to introduce and explore the story of creation
- to understand that all of creation—and all good things that come from creation—are gifts to us from God
- to deepen our sense of wonder, gratitude and respect for all God's gifts to us
- to recognize our role as stewards (not owners) of God's gifts

Activities
- Story: Creation
- Checking In
- Giving Box
- Stewardship Prayer
- Art Response
- Second Story: David, Solomon and the Temple
- Field Trip
- Around the Table
- Music
- Praying Together

Scripture Summary
God creates the world, bringing order out of chaos, light and beauty out of darkness and confusion. God entrusts the care of creation to humans, not only giving them all good things to enjoy, but also holding them responsible to care for and share this great gift.

Scripture Background

This reading is the first of the two accounts of creation in Genesis. Though it appears first in the Bible, most scholars think that this account was actually composed after the exile (around 400 B.C.) when the Bible as we have it today was being assembled. It is a master stroke to use this as the beginning of the Bible because of its lofty theology of an all-powerful and sovereign God. By placing this at the beginning, everything else in the Bible will be interpreted through this portrait of God.

In solemn liturgical cadences, the priestly writer describes how darkness and chaos give way to light and order at God's command. Rather than simply producing things from nothing, God brings order into creation so that everything has its proper place and is in the right relationship with everything else. Time (the seven days, daylight and darkness) and space (sky, sea and dry land) and all the various creatures proper to each realm are organized by the creative word of God. Always the writer echoes the refrain, "God was pleased with what he saw" (vv. 4, 10, 12, 18, 21, 25), "very pleased" (v. 31).

On the sixth and final day of creating things, God says, "Now we will make human beings" (v. 26). "Human beings," a collective singular noun without indication of number or gender, are created in God's image and likeness, to enter into relationship with God and to be God's representatives on earth. Then God gives creation and its care into the hands of the human beings (vv. 29-30) who will share in God's dominion over creation to make sure that everything remains in the right relationships that God has established.

Creation is not only a gift for "human beings" but also a responsibility. Dominion does not simply mean that we are able to ruthlessly use the goods of creation but that we are to be "masters" (Latin, *dominus*) over creation according to the image of God the Creator. Our task, like that of God and the master of any household, demands providing for those under our care and protecting them from harm. We are called upon to use the goods of the earth according to the order God has established.

Chapter 4, Session 2: Creation

Our stewardship over creation is based on a gift and requires a responsibility. Good stewardship is good ordering of the gifts of creation according to God's guidelines so that God might look down upon our works and be "very pleased."

Reflection and Response

When we read the Genesis account of human origins, it becomes crystal clear that everything we are and everything we have is a direct gift from God. And God was certainly not stingy with us, providing abundant water, fruitful plants, lights at night, creatures of sea and land, even a human companion to offset loneliness.

If we are indeed made in the divine image (1:27), should we not respond to the gifts of creation in kind? We cannot create the stars or the ocean, but we can appreciate them. Everything in nature bears in some varied way the distinctive marks of the Creator, but how often do we pause to look for that signature? Do we build on our children's delight in the natural world, or entertain them with mind-numbing television programs, violent video games, and the malls or amusement parks which a greed-driven culture has determined are "fun"?

Perhaps one simple step towards responsible stewardship would be to take ourselves and our children on regular walks outdoors, where we marvel at the insect kingdom, spring or autumn leaves, a brook, a sunset, a puddle or the night sky. It's simple, it's free, and it plants the first seeds of religious faith: awe and wonder at creation. Full-throated praise of the Creator must spring from personal experience. We can't invent it or fake it.

Such experiences with God's artistry seem essential to an authentic life of faith. Without them, religious exercises in a stuffy room become boring and hollow routines. Cut off from the natural world, we worship with all the vigor of a sickly hothouse tomato. Genuine sacramental life makes abundant use of created elements: water, oil, fire, incense, bread and wine, ashes, flowers, images of eagles, lions, oxen, snakes and doves. Jesus spoke warmly of vines and branches, lilies in the field, sparrows and vineyards. His teaching was firmly grounded in the lakes, hills, roads and gardens of Galilee. If we and our children respect the earth as the beautiful home God

designed, we might be less likely to exploit natural resources, more likely to protect them reverently, recycle, and restrain our greed.

Often, the most admirable kinds of stewardship flourish in the most unlikely locales. Read, for instance, Jonathon Kozol's book *Ordinary Resurrections* about St. Ann's Episcopal Church in the South Bronx. In a dangerous setting, against deadly odds, Mother Martha and her staff run an after-school program to protect and nurture neighborhood children. Courageous and caring, they provide snacks, homework help and listening ears to children who struggle daily with hunger, asthma, limited opportunity, family members in jail, "dreams deferred" and what Kozol calls the "abominations of...apartheid, separate and unequal schools."

Similar programs flourish around the country. Many churches sponsor dining rooms where the hungry and homeless are fed in dignity, with candles, fresh flowers and clean linen on the tables. Other churches that practice stewardship channel funds to much-needed relief work in Haiti, Africa or Asia. Through works like these, the Creator is praised and all creation is blessed.

Read through the scripture passage. Quietly consider:
■ For which gifts of God am I most deeply grateful?

_____

_____

_____

_____

_____

_____

_____

_____

My Own Story
Gratitude or Attitude?
■ Our families of origin set the foundation for how we view nature, possessions and the circumstances of our lives. What tone did you experience growing up?

To what extent was it one of *gratitude* ("We've been blessed with so much. Look around and see the good things God has given us. Count your blessings; name them one by one. My glass is always half full.") and what to extent was it one of *entitlement* ("The world owes us this. I've worked for everything I've gotten. My glass is always half empty.")?

■ At what points in your life, either as a child or an adult, have you been particularly aware of God's goodness to you? What triggered these experiences?

■ What two or three individuals in your life have modeled gratitude for you, helping you to see the glass as "half full"?

■ In what ways have you *learned* gratitude over the years? How do you express it today, both personally, and within your family?

_____

_____

_____

_____

_____

_____

_____

_____

_____

Creation

■ During your childhood, what memories do you have about the natural world? How much time did your family spend outdoors? What were your favorite outdoor activities?

■ As a child, in what ways were you taught to care for the created world? to make use of nature? to appreciate nature?

■ At what age do you first remember a strong "connection" to something in creation? a sense of awe or wonder at the natural world? As an adult, when do you experience a personal connection to God's love through creation?

■ For some people, the word *environmentalism* carries negative associations. As an adult, what have you observed about the environmental movement? What part have you played in it? How would you define "biblical environmentalism"?

■ Since you've had your own family, how have you attempted to convey to your children appreciation and care for the natural world?

■ What natural places are sacred and renewing for you?

_____

_____

_____

_____

_____

_____

_____

Chapter 4, Session 2: Creation

Story: Creation

Soon after your child hears the story of Creation in the session at church, review the story together, perhaps at the conclusion of a meal or just before bedtime. Children appreciate repetition, so don't hesitate to repeat the story several times, perhaps choosing several different approaches throughout the week.

Story Options

☐ *Child's Storytelling*
Invite your child to tell you the story of Creation as he or she recalls it from the session at church.

☐ *Children's Paper*
Look together at the Children's Paper that your child brought home from church. Grades 1-2 could read the story to the family, perhaps at the conclusion of a meal together. Children in grades 3-6 could read the story directly from the Bible.

☐ *Children's Bible*
Read together the story of Creation from a children's Bible or Bible storybook.

☐ *Children's Books*
Read one of the following books together:
— *Creation* by Laurie Lazzara Knowlton (Torrance, CA: Grace Publications, 1997)
— *What Next?* by Mary Manz Simon (St. Louis, MO: Concordia, 1990)
— *When the Beginning Began: Stories about God, the Creatures, and Us* by Julius Lester (New York: Silver Whistle, 1999)

Checking In 〰〰〰〰〰

Discover what your child *really* thinks about the gifts God has given us. Here are several activities to help children express themselves. Remember, no matter what responses you might get—even ones that surprise you—

affirm all answers, respect your child's feelings and opinions, and occasionally restate what your child says to make sure you've understood.

Check-In Options

☐ *Quick Sketch*
Give every family member a piece of drawing paper and a pencil (or crayons, felt markers, etc.). Ask everyone to draw a quick picture of creation. Allow just 1 minute before asking everyone to show and explain their drawings.

☐ *Family Talk—Creation*
Discuss the following questions, being certain to share your answers as well:
— In the story you heard at church this week, what did you learn about God? about God's big world? about all the things that God made?
— Of all the things that God created, which ones are your favorites?
— Of all the things that *you* create, which ones are your favorites?
— You are God's creation, too! What makes *you* a good part of God's creation?

☐ *Graffiti Page*
In the center of a large sheet of light-colored construction paper, newsprint or poster board, write the word *CREATION*. Make available felt markers or crayons and invite family members to gather around the paper and to add words, drawings and phrases about creation to the paper, filling it with words and images. When finished, discuss: "What does our graffiti say about creation? about God's good gifts to us?"

Giving Box 〰〰〰〰〰〰〰

For a complete description of the Giving Box, along with suggestions for its use, see Session One, page 21. We offer two new suggestions below.

Giving Box Options

☐ *Gift Box*

This week make your Giving Box into a "Gift Box": Make available slips of paper and pens or pencils. Each evening this week, invite each family member to write or draw one gift God has given them for which they are especially grateful: toys, friends, other family members, abilities, pets, rainfall, sunshine, etc. As each slip is placed in the box, the family member can pray, "Thank you, God, for the gift of...." Other family members can respond: "Thank you, God, for all your gifts."

☐ *Sharing Box*

Your Giving Box could also become a "Sharing Box" this week: Each day, invite family members to write or draw a way in which they could share with someone else that day (or the next day). For example, a child could draw the sharing of a toy; a teen could write about spending time with a hurting friend; a parent could consider a way to help out a stressed coworker. Dropping these slips into the Sharing Box helps solidify family members' intentions.

Stewardship Prayer 〰️

In the sessions at church, some children are learning this prayer, repeating it every week at the conclusion of their session. You could also use the prayer at home throughout the four weeks of *Growing a Grateful, Generous Heart*. See the *Options* following the prayer.

Prayer

Thank you, Jesus, for bringing us together in
your love.
Thank you for giving us everything we need.
Help us to take good care of the gifts you've
given us.
Help us to use them to do your work. *Amen.*

Stewardship Prayer Options

☐ *Prayer Poster*

If you created the Prayer Poster last week (p. 21), use it as you continue to pray the Stewardship Prayer.

☐ *Prayer Booklet*

If you began the Prayer Booklet project last week (p. 22), add to it this week.

☐ *Discussion*

As a family, explore more of the prayer's meaning. You could ask:
— Of all the good gifts God gives us, which are your favorites?
— What good gifts has God given us today?
— What could we thank God for right now?

☐ *Sing the Prayer*

Put the prayer to music. Together think of a tune for a children's song that might fit the words, or invite children to create their own tune.

Art Response 〰️

Complete one or more of the art projects suggested below. Remember, the goal is not the final product, but the time spent together exploring the Bible story and learning about each other.

Art Options

☐ *Creation Poems*

Together write poems celebrating creation. Here's a suggested poem structure:

first line: a noun (person, place or thing)
second line: two adjectives describing the noun
third line: three verbs related to the noun
fourth line: an idea or thought (Could be a short
sentence.)
fifth line: repeat the first line

Here's a sample poem, using as the noun something chosen from creation:

Tree
Green, leafy
Shades, rustles, cools
I fall asleep underneath
Tree

Creation Slide Show

Using a digital camera, a computer and basic photo software, make a Creation Slide Show. Together take pictures illustrating the six days of creation (around the house or in the neighborhood). Download the photos to the computer and arrange them in order using your photo software. Depending on how much time (and expertise) you have, you could add captions, music and/or narration. Note that many older children and teens may already have the skills to put this together, even if you, as a parent, do not.

Option: Instead of illustrating the creation story, ask each family member to take 10 digital pictures of his or her favorite gifts from God. Combine these into your Slide Show.

Option: If you don't have access to a digital camera or computer, give each family member an inexpensive, 12-shot, disposable camera and give them 48 hours to take pictures to combine into a Photo Show (instead of a Slide Show). Combine these photos into a simple album, with captions written by family members to describe their favorite gifts from God.

No matter which option you choose, include photos of you and your children—you too are gifts from God!

Nature Mobile
Gather natural materials found in the neighborhood (leaves, sticks, rocks, twigs) and combine them into a mobile to hang somewhere in your

Second Story: David, Solomon and the Temple

For older children, it can be revealing to link scripture stories with similar themes. This week, if you wish, explore the story of David as he turns over his kingship to his son Solomon and prepares Solomon to build God's Temple. In the first portion of the passage, 1 Chronicles 28:1–29:9, David tells why he won't be building the Temple (God wants Solomon to do it) and urges Solomon and the people of Israel to remain faithful to God and enjoy the land God has given them. Then, starting in 1 Chronicles 29:10-19, David offers a remarkable speech praising God for God's generosity, concluding by telling God, "...my people and I cannot really give you anything, because everything is a gift from you, and we have only given back what is yours already" (v. 14). This verse is frequently used in worship services when the offering is brought forward.

Read this story, starting with 1 Chronicles 28:1–29:9. Discuss:

- Describe David. What kind of person was he?
- Describe David's son, Solomon. What kind of person was he?
- What big project was Solomon going to be working on?

Read 1 Chronicles 29:10-22. Discuss:
- According to David, where do all good things come from? *(You might also read 1 Timothy 4:4-5.)*
- To whom do all these good gifts really belong?
- How does David respond to God's good gifts?
- How can *we* respond to God's good gifts?

Feel free to adapt any other activity from these sessions to explore the story further (like having children retell the story, act out the story or illustrate the story with a family mural).

home. Two crossed sticks (each about 2' long) can be lashed together to form an "X"; this provides the frame. Hang items from the frame, balancing them so that the frame hangs evenly. If you take the Nature Walk described below under Field Trip, the items collected could be used for the Nature Mobile.

Around the Table 〰〰〰

Family mealtimes, either at home or out, can be a great place to continue exploring the weekly themes of *Growing a Grateful, Generous Heart.*

Table Options

☐ *Family Talk–Gifts*

Discuss the following questions, being certain to share your answers as well:

- God gives us all of creation to enjoy. What do you like best in God's big world?
- If you had been in charge of creating everything, what else would you have made?
- People are God's creation too, including *you.* Let's name people who are great gifts to us.
- Why do you think God gives us so many good gifts?
- What good gifts from God could we share with others?

☐ *Gratitude Dinner*

When the family gathers for a meal, talk about how one item of food got to your table. See how long a "gratitude list" you can come up with while enjoying that item. For example, as you share bread or rolls, consider:

- What went into the creation of the bread? seeds? rain? the warmth of the sun? butter from a cow? an egg from a chicken? salt and sugar from other countries?
- Who helped along the way? farmers growing grain, collecting eggs or milking cows? truck drivers who transported the ingredients? a worker in a bakery or grocery store? someone at home who made the bread?
- Who else helped make it possible for you to enjoy the bread? How about those who made the truck

that carried the ingredients? those who produce the electricity coming to the store so it could sell it to you?

☐ *I Spy*

Play a version of "I Spy." One family member is *It. It* picks something nearby for other family members to guess and says, "I spy a gift from God, and it's blue *(or some other characteristic of the object)."* Family members guess until someone guesses correctly. The one who guesses correctly is the next *It.*

Field Trip 〰〰〰

Plan to take your family on an outing to experience, explore and share creation.

Field Trip Options

☐ *Nature Walk*

Take a Nature Walk around the neighborhood, in a local park or somewhere farther afield, like a riverbank, woods or meadow. Invite each family member to collect six or more "natural treasures": a colorful stone, a bird's feather, a unique leaf, a piece of bark, a seed pod, etc. Make a display of these items at home and talk about what you like most in nature. Items could be glued to a poster titled *God's Great Gifts*; decorate the poster with other nature pictures. (See Other Resources in Chapter 3, p. 14, for books on helping children explore nature.)

☐ *Museum or Nature Preserve*

Visit a natural history museum, bird sanctuary or other nature site. Many offer interactive exhibits created just for kids. Explore and talk about God's amazing world, and what parts of the attraction each family member found most fascinating.

☐ *Use Your Senses*

Visit a favorite "nature spot." Use your five senses to explore creation:

- Sit in silence and *listen,* then discuss: "What different sounds do we hear?"

— Sit in silence and *smell*, then discuss: "What different scents do we smell? Do we smell something sweet? salty? pungent? rotten?"

— Sit in silence and *look*, then discuss: "What new things do we see? What colors? shapes?"

— Sit in silence and *touch*, then discuss: "What textures are nearby us? How does a stick feel? dirt? sand? stones? water? leaves? our skin? Which things are rough? smooth? bumpy? sticky? dry?"

— If you're careful, you could also sit in silence and *taste*. We suggest breaking a pine needle or leaf stem and touching it to the tongue. (Skip this one if you're concerned about health issues.) Discuss: "What do they taste like? salty? bitter? sweet?"

— Discuss: "Why do you think God gave us so many senses? Which is your favorite? Of all the things we've heard, smelled, seen, touched (and tasted), which was your favorite? Which did you like the least? What would you like to say to God right now about God's great gift of creation?"

Music

If your family sings together, learn and enjoy the song "Friends with God," found on page 24. The four verses of the song correspond to the four sessions of *Growing a Grateful, Generous Heart.* This week, review the first verse and chorus, then together learn the second verse.

Music Options

☐ *New Verses*
Try writing new verses for "Friends with God" that list the gifts of God for which family members are grateful, for example:

Thank you, God, for Gramma,
and thank you, God, for cats.
Thank you for Nintendo
and different colored hats.

☐ *Actions*
Invite family members to make up actions to accompany the verses of "Friends with God" learned so far.

Praying Together

There are as many ways to pray as there are people who pray. Each week we'll suggest a few ideas to choose from, or you may wish to use those from other sessions. You can always combine prayer methods as well.

Prayer Options

☐ *Gifts Ritual*
— Gather the family. Give each person 5 minutes to gather 5 items from around the house (and yard) for which he or she is particularly grateful.
— When everyone returns, set a candle on a low table and place the gathered items around it. Talk about the items: "How are these gifts from God?"
— Light the candle. Take turns completing this prayer: "Thank you, God, for the gift of..." Everyone respond: "Thank you, God, for all your gifts." Complete the prayer using the names of family members: "Thank you, God, for the gift of Alyce."
— Close by saying *"Amen"* in unison.

☐ *Word Association Prayer*
— Someone begins by naming a good gift in God's creation, for example: *sunshine.*
— Other family members respond with words suggested by the first word: *light, warm, summer...*
— Let a different family member introduce the next gift. Continue for many of God's good gifts.

☐ *Prayer Book*
From *The Book of Common Prayer*, pray the Collect "for stewardship of creation" (19, III, p. 259).

☐ *Psalm Prayer*
Pray Psalm 19:1-6 (identifying God's glory in creation), all or part of Psalm 104 (praising God as Creator) or Psalm 148 (calling on creation to praise God).

☐ *Prayer Song*
Sing "Friends with God" (p. 24), or from *The Hymnal 1982* either "Joyful, joyful we adore thee," (#376) or "For the beauty of the earth," (#416).

☐ *Stewardship Prayer*
Learn and pray the Stewardship Prayer, found on page 21.

SESSION 3 The Widow's Offering

Part One: FOR PARENTS

Scripture
Mark 12:38-44

Theme
Our greatest joy is to give back to God and others.

Objectives
- to model the widow's trust and generosity
- to discover practical ways to give to God and others
- to motivate us to share the good gifts God gives us

Activities
- Story: The Widow's Offering
- Checking In
- Giving Box
- Stewardship Prayer
- Around the Table
- Art Response
- Second Story: The Rich Man and Jesus
- Field Trip
- Music
- Praying Together

Scripture Summary
While teaching in the Temple, Jesus first warns against the pretense and pride of the teachers of the law, who take advantage of the poor and make a show of their wealth and prestige, then points to the contrasting example of the widow, who, trusting in God's love and care, gives all the money she has to help others.

Scripture Background

This reading is the final public teaching of Jesus in Mark's gospel. It concludes a series of heated controversies between Jesus and the Jerusalem authorities (12:13-44) that illustrate the difference between Jesus' new way of understanding and relating to God and the old way prescribed by the Jewish leaders. Jesus' primary emphasis focuses on God's generosity and our thankfulness instead of the popular Jewish emphasis on God's holiness and our legal observance.

In dialogue with the wealthy Sadducees, the scholarly scribes and the zealous Pharisees, Jesus offers fresh alternatives for understanding his teaching authority, paying taxes to the Romans who were occupying their country, the possibility of resurrection, the identity of the Messiah and generous giving to support the temple.

Although Jesus related positively to individual scribes (12:34), these controversies reveal his radical challenge to the Jewish religious way of living. They also echo the situation of Mark's community when the early Church was differentiating itself from a Judaism grown defensive after the fall of the temple in the year 70. The negative example of the greedy and conniving scribes is contrasted with a poor widow's sincere generosity to the temple. The two incidents are linked by the word *widow* (12:40, 42).

Jesus strongly condemns the scribes or scholars of the law for their duplicity and hypocrisy. Outwardly they seek honors and embrace the trappings of religious practices and public prayers. But inwardly they are motivated by greed and use their knowledge of the technicalities of the Mosaic law to appropriate for their own use the "houses" and wealth of defenseless widows.

In contrast to their corruption, Jesus offers the example of another widow who has come to the temple to make an offering. Her self-giving is a reversal of the self-serving of the scribes. Without fanfare, the widow gives out of her need rather than out of her surplus, offering her emptiness to God—an emptiness that indicates her capacity to be filled. Good stewardship is sincere and generous giving, sharing the much or little that we have out of love rather than duty or reward.

Chapter 4, Session 2: Creation

Reflection and Response

The widow in today's readings is a painful reminder of human vulnerability. While few of us have been reduced to the dire straits of two coins, we recognize in our moments of scorching honesty how all that is most precious to us could be wiped out in seconds.

The Middle Eastern widow has not vanished from our concern. Just as she haunted the margins of Jesus' society, so she crosses our newswire services today. Labeled "collateral damage" as American soldiers marched toward Baghdad, she wept for soldiers killed in both Iraq wars.

In a joint statement February 20, 2003, Archbishop of Canterbury Rowan Williams and Catholic Cardinal O'Connor of England cautioned about "unpredictable humanitarian consequences of a war with Iraq." Surely one consequence is the widow who has no means of support in a society that frowns on women working. Beneath her black burka, she holds the Palestinian child maimed by an Israeli raid. Lighting the Hannukah candles, she mourns the husband killed by a suicide bomber on a Jerusalem bus.

Stark poverty is nasty for those who experience it, but secondarily for those who observe. It raises the uncomfortable question of whether we all aren't one illness, one car repair, or one downsizing away from that state ourselves. But our empathy halts when she drops her last coins into the collection box. Never, ever could we do that—we are, we harrumph, fiscally responsible. As Edwina Gateley writes in *Soul Sisters*, addressing the widow who gave the mite: "Poverty did not suck dry the richness of your spirit, sister! It could not squeeze small your generous heart, but left you rich in wisdom."

What do we do before such generosity? How do we respond when we are dared to model such trust? Do we answer the call to become like God, pouring out in abundance all our resources of time, energy or money? And like good stewards, do we guard our own wobbly security, know when we've reached our limits, care for the caregiver when it becomes vital?

Those who are a bit troubled by the widow can find good news in recent interpretations of this gospel.

Scholars see it now not so much as a "quaint vignette about the superior piety of the poor," but as a scathing criticism of the system that exploits them.

We see this principle personified when Jesus takes his seat facing the temple treasury. As Ched Myers points out in *Binding the Strong Man,* the stage direction indicates judgment, for Jesus will shortly face the temple to predict its imminent destruction.

At the time Jesus leveled his criticism, the scribes administered widows' estates. Their compensation was a percentage of the assets, which led to widespread abuse. Rather than extending traditional protection to the widow and orphan, the system exploited them. Myers concludes, "The temple has robbed this woman of her very means of livelihood...As if in disgust, Jesus 'exits' the temple—for the final time."

He leaves the corrupt state of Judaism to establish a new order. He was on his way to the cross, to lay down his life for those who had been trampled upon by religious codes and authorities. In his action we can sense the futility of both human systems—the Church Christ founded would replicate many of Judaism's abuses.

Thus, Christ intervenes for us on a plane beyond human tragedy. We are no longer merely driftwood tossed by continuous catastrophes. The world's widows and orphans (and all who are spiritually or emotionally orphaned) have their own high priest, who for love of them gives everything.

Read through the scripture passage. Quietly consider:
- What's my response to the model of the widow in today's story?

_____

_____

_____

_____

_____

_____

_____

_____

Chapter 4, Session 3: The Widow's Offering

My Own Story

Giving

- What are your early memories of giving? Do you remember the offering plate being passed at church? What did you put in the plate? Where did the money come from? your parents? your allowance? What feelings do you associate with giving?

- How were "stewardship" and "giving" regarded in your home? as a burden? a privilege? a joy? What expectations do you recall about giving to others? helping others?

- At what point do you remember "owning" the act of "giving"? In other words, when were you aware of giving money (or time or possessions) because you wanted to, not because it was part of the routine or expected of you? What motivated your giving?

- What does giving mean to you today? In what different ways do you give to others? In what ways does giving become a (possibly painful) sacrifice, as it may have been for the widow in today's story? In what ways does your personal giving reflect your trust in God?

- How do you communicate your beliefs about giving and stewardship to your children?

_____

_____

_____

_____

_____

_____

_____

_____

_____

_____

How Much Is Enough?

- Today's story (the Widow's Offering), along with the Second Story suggested later in this session (the Rich Man and Jesus), challenge those of us living comfortably in one of the world's richest nations.
  - What's your initial reaction to either or both of these stories? How do you feel? What's your first thought?
  - What do you hear God asking of *you* in these stories? What might God be asking of *your family*?
  - What "two little copper coins" do you have to offer God? How do you give them?
  - in what ways can you follow through on Jesus' injunction to "sell all you have and give the money to the poor"?
  - Given our current responsibilities and needs, what, in practical terms, might God be asking of us today?

- Make a two-column chart on a blank piece of paper. Title the first column *Enough* and the second column *More Than Enough*. Spend some time listing items in both columns: in the first column list what really would be enough (for you to survive, to have your needs met) in various areas of your life, for example, food, shelter, clothing, possessions, etc.; in the second column list items that you might want or enjoy, but that really represent "more than enough." When you're done, spend time reflecting on what you've written: How might the widow in today's story respond to your list? the rich man? Jesus?

_____

_____

_____

_____

_____

_____

_____

_____

_____

_____

Story: The Widow's Offering

Soon after your child hears the story of the Widow's Offering in the session at church, review the story together, perhaps at the conclusion of a meal or just before bedtime. Children appreciate repetition, so don't hesitate to repeat the story several times, perhaps choosing several different approaches throughout the week.

Story Options

☐ *Child's Storytelling*

Invite your child to tell you the story of the Widow's Offering as he or she recalls it from the week's session at church.

☐ *Children's Paper*

Look together at the Children's Paper that your child brought home from the session at Church. Children in grades 1-2 could read the story to the family, perhaps at the conclusion of a meal together. Children in grades 3-6 could read the story directly from the Bible.

☐ *Children's Bible*

Read together the story of the Widow's Offering from a children's Bible or Bible storybook.

☐ *Your Family Version*

Invite all family members to retell the story of the Widow's Offering, imagining what more there might be to the story, for example:

— What did the widow do that morning before she came to the Temple? Was she with her children? her best friend? What did they talk about? Where did her two coins come from?

— What was the widow feeling as she prepared to give her money? Was she humming cheerfully to herself? wondering if she should give both coins or only one?

— What did the widow do after she left the Temple? Did she stop to say hello to Jesus? stop by to visit a friend?

Checking In

Discover what your child *really* thinks about giving to others. Here are several activities to help children express themselves. Remember, no matter what responses you might get—even ones that surprise you—affirm all answers, respect your child's feelings and opinions, and occasionally restate what your child says to make sure you've understood.

Check-In Options

☐ *Clay Play*

Open up a package of modeling clay and invite family members to sculpt their responses to today's story. If they need further encouragement, you could suggest:

— Make the two coins the woman gave.

— Sculpt how it feels to give to others.

— Create something about giving.

When family members have finished, invite them to show and explain their sculptures.

☐ *Family Talk—$1 Million*

Let each family member explain what they would do if they won money. Start by asking:

— If you won $5, how would you spend it? What if you won $10? How about $100? $1,000? $1 million?

— If you were given $5, *but you had to give it away,* to whom would you give it? What if you had to give away $10? $100? $1,000? $1 million?

☐ *Family Talk—The Ways We Give*

Explore with family members the various ways they give to or share with others:

— What was the last gift you gave to someone? *or* When today did you share with someone? (Note: The things we give to share with others may be nonmaterial, like a hug or time spent listening. You might suggest these or similar examples as you identify ways that family members give to others.)*

Chapter 4, Session 3: The Widow's Offering

- What do you think your gift meant to the person who received it?
- How did you feel, giving (or sharing) this gift?
- When does giving (or sharing) feel good? When might giving (or sharing) be hard to do?

Giving Box ∿∿∿∿∿∿∿∿

For a complete description of the Giving Box, along with suggestions for its use, see Session 1, page 21 and Session 2, pages 30-31. Below are two additional suggestions:

Giving Box Options

☐ *Family Talk—Our Gift Box and the Widow's Offering*
Explore the close tie between your Giving Box and today's story. You might discuss:
- In what ways is our Giving Box like the Temple treasury in today's story?
- In what ways are the widow's two little copper coins like the money (or slips of paper) we've put into our Giving Box?

☐ *Family Talk—Donating Our Gifts*
If you've been putting money into your Giving Box and haven't yet chosen a recipient, decide together whom you'd like to give the money to, once you've completed the four weeks of *Growing a Grateful, Generous Heart.* You might ask:
- To whom could we give the money in our Giving Box?
- What do we hope the money would do for the people who receive it?

Stewardship Prayer ∿∿∿∿∿∿

In the sessions at church, some children are learning this prayer, repeating it every week at the conclusion of their session. You could also use the prayer at home through-out the four weeks of *Growing a Grateful, Generous Heart.* See the *Options* following the prayer.

Prayer

Thank you, Jesus, for bringing us together in your love.
Thank you for giving us everything we need.
Help us to take good care of the gifts you've given us.
Help us to use them to do your work. *Amen.*

Stewardship Prayer Options

☐ *Prayer Poster*
If you created the Prayer Poster in Session 1 (p. 21), use it as you continue to pray the Stewardship Prayer.

☐ *Prayer Booklet*
If you began the Prayer Booklet project in Session 1 (p. 22), add to it this week.

☐ *Discussion*
As a family, explore more of the prayer's meaning. You could ask:
- In our Stewardship Prayer we say to God, "Help us to use [the gifts you give us] to do your work." What "work" of God could we do with the gifts God has given us? *(If necessary, be more specific, for example, "What 'work' of God could we do with our allowance money? with our time with friends? How could we help others with our toys and games? with our ability to run? to jump? to tell jokes?)*
- How can we "take good care" of the things God has given us? *(for example, bikes, brothers and sisters, good health, forests and rivers)*

☐ *Praying with Movement*
Invite family members to make up movements for each line of the prayer. Do the movements together as you pray the prayer. Movements will make the prayer easier to remember.

Around the Table ∿∿∿∿∿∿

Family mealtimes, either at home or out, can be a great place to explore the themes of *Growing a Grateful, Generous Heart.*

Chapter 4, Session 3: The Widow's Offering

Table Options

☐ *Family Talk—Giving*

Discuss the following questions, being certain to share your answers as well:
— What makes something a good gift?
— If you could give each person here any one gift— no matter how much it cost or how hard it was to get—what would you give?
— What one special thing that you own would be the *hardest* to give away? Why would it be hard to give that thing away?

Discuss these questions with older children:
— Think again of that item that would be the hardest to give away: What would it take for you to be willing to give it away? To whom would you give it?
— What does the word *sacrifice* mean? *(giving that results in a sense of loss)* When have you had to sacrifice? How did that feel? What was the result? As you look back on your sacrifice, how do you feel about it now?
— In what ways do you believe God calls us to sacrifice for others?

☐ *Widow/Rich Man Roleplay*

If you have discussed the alternate scripture story (see Second Story, below), then spend a few minutes roleplaying a conversation between the widow who offered her two copper coins and the rich man who went away sad when faced with Jesus' challenge to sell all he had and give the money to the poor. Ask one family member to take the part of *the widow* and another to take the part of *the rich man*. You could pretend that they are having dinner together, and sharing their thoughts and feelings about money, God, trust, lifestyle and faith. The younger the participants, the simpler the discussion will need to be. Here are a few suggestions for getting started:
— *(For the widow:)* Why did you give your two coins? Was that *really* all you had?
— *(For the rich man:)* Why did you leave Jesus feeling sad? Couldn't you have sold *some* stuff and given the money to the poor?
— *(For both:)* Tell us what you think about God. Tell us what you believe about how God cares for you. Tell us how you show your trust in God.

Note: If you did *not* look at the story of the rich man, ask one family member to pretend to be the widow in today's story. Ask to hear the story from the widow's perspective, and ask additional questions of the widow:
— How could you give away *everything*? Aren't you worried about where your next meal is coming from?
— Did you get a chance to talk to Jesus? What did he say to you?

Art Response

Complete one or more of the art projects suggested below. Remember, the goal is not the final product, but the time spent together exploring the Bible story and learning about each other and yourselves.

Art Options

☐ *Kitchen Gifts*

As a family, work together to prepare a food gift to share with someone in need. First talk about who could use a food gift this week and what they might need or enjoy. Is there someone in your parish going through a difficult time, perhaps dealing with an illness or recent death? Consider delivering a complete, hot meal. Or a plate of homemade, hand-decorated cookies could bring joy to a parish shut-in. Together buy the ingredients, prepare the food, create a card of encouragement, pack everything up with a decorative ribbon and deliver it. Spending time with the recipients will make the activity even more meaningful. And while you're there, are there other ways you could help, doing laundry, cleaning up the kitchen or running an errand?

Note: A food gift is only one of several projects you could undertake as a family. Someone at your parish may suggest other options, or simply look to what family members do best. For example, if your family loves to hike or bike, perhaps a harried single parent would welcome a break from childcare; invite his or her kids to join you for an afternoon of hiking or biking. Are you a handy-person? Undertake a project for someone who needs a home repair. The point? Find a way to help others that offers hands-on involvement for everyone in your family.

☐ *Stewardship Posters*
Create an acrostic "Stewardship Poster" for your family. Start with a large sheet of poster board. Across the top write *We Are All...* Then, down the left side, in large letters, write the word *STEWARDS*. Working together, think of eight ways in which you and your family can share with others (or each other) some of the great gifts God has given you. Begin each of these ways with one of the letters in the word STEWARDS. Your list might begin something like this:

Share a family dinner this week with our new neighbors
Take the box of clothes to Goodwill
Eat my lunch with the new kid in my class who's alone every day
Watch Kiki's favorite video with her (for the umpteenth time)
(Etc.)

Make every suggestion practical and do-able. Suggestions might apply to the entire family or to a single family member. Be creative and have fun. Use available art materials to decorate the poster, for example, tearing and gluing shapes from construction paper, outlining the first letters of each line with

Second Story:
The Rich Man and Jesus

Especially for older children, it can be challenging and revealing to link scripture stories with similar themes. This week, if you wish, explore the story of the rich Jewish leader who asks Jesus about eternal life. Though an earnest seeker, he decides (unlike the widow) that the cost of following God's way asks more of him than he's willing to give. Below, we use the story as it appears in Mark 10:17-22, but you'll find the same story, with slight variations, in Matthew 19:16-30 and Luke 18:18-30.

Read this story with your children, starting with Mark 10:17-22. Discuss:
▪ Describe the rich man. What is he hoping for? What kind of life has he lived?
 ▪ What does Jesus tell the rich man to do? Would this be an easy thing to do or a hard thing to do? Why?
 ▪ Why do you think Jesus wants us to share what we have with the poor?

How does the rich man feel?
▪ What do you think the rich man might have done next?
▪ Imagine that the widow from today's other story and the rich man from this story had lunch together. What might they have talked about?

Read Mark 10:23-31. Discuss:
▪ What does Jesus say that surprises the disciples?
▪ Why do you think it's hard for a rich person to enter God's Kingdom?
▪ Who makes it possible for anyone—rich or poor—to enter God's Kingdom?
▪ Why might *we* want to share God's great gifts with others?

Feel free to adapt any other activity from these sessions to explore the story further (like having children retell the story, act out the story or illustrate the story with a family mural).

glue and sprinkling on glitter, or tearing out and gluing on pictures from magazines. Throughout the week, as each item is completed, check it off and celebrate it together with a cheer, a song, a prayer and/or the lighting of a special candle.

☐ *"Coin" Gift Certificates*
Family members can create "gift certificates" to distribute to friends, neighbors or each other. First invite every family member to think of two ways in which they could give to (help) someone else, for example:
— baby-sitting for an evening
— raking a lawn
— cooking a meal
— playing a game
— going for a walk
— sharing a favorite toy
— doing a chore
— giving a 10-minute shoulder rub

Each of these gifts will be written on a coin-shaped "gift certificate" to be redeemed by the recipient. Coins could be cut from heavy cardboard (4"-6" circles) and covered with foil. Permanent markers (for example, Sharpies) will write on the foil. Or cover the cardboard circles with yellow construction paper and write on them with regular felt markers. You could also cover round sandwich cookies (for example, Oreos) with foil and attach tags identifying the promised "gifts." Possible text for the certificates could be:
— This coin entitles the bearer to three games of their choice. Redeemable anytime.
— Good for 3 hours of baby-sitting by Janice. Just say when!

You could decorate the coins with additional designs like those found on real coins. Consider adding the reference for today's story of the Widow's Offering– Mark 12:38-44.

When finished, encourage family members to hand deliver their completed coins, and, of course, to follow through on their gifts.

Field Trip

Take your family on an outing to experience the joy of sharing with others.

Field Trip Options

☐ *Grocery Shopping*
Take your children grocery shopping. As you shop, pick out items to donate as well as items for your family. You could, for example, agree to select one item to donate for every 10 items for the family. Allow children to make selections as well. Once home, put the items to be donated together in a box. Arrange to take these items to a local food bank or needy family–and deliver together. (Someone at your parish should be able to direct you to organizations or people in need of your donation.)

☐ *Helping-Hand Bags*
If your community is one of many in America where homelessness is a problem, prepare "Helping-Hand Bags" to hand out to people on the street. Into paper lunch sacks, place several items that may be of value to someone who was homeless, for example, a box of juice, a granola bar or fruit bar, homemade cookies, wrapped cheese, a piece of fruit, bus tokens or coupons, a pair of new socks, a gift certificate to a local restaurant, information on a local shelter or food bank, etc. Take time as a family to distribute these. With you by their side, let the children have the experience of handing out the bags. Show respect to those you are serving, introducing yourselves and talking to them. Such experiences can profoundly affect both you and your children.

☐ *Volunteering*
As a family, volunteer to help somewhere in your community. Your church may already have programs feeding the hungry, offering day care, providing shelter or in some other way serving the needy. If not, someone at your church likely will be able to direct you to community agencies who could use your help. Hands-on experiences, with one-on-one contact with those being helped, have the potential for lasting impact on those doing the helping.

☐ *Closet Search*

Ask family members to go through their closets and drawers and each to find five personal items to give away, including clothes, toys, jewelry, kitchen items, tools, books, tapes or CDs, videos, etc. Regather and review what people have brought. Together discuss:

— Why did you pick these items? Which are easy to give away? Which are harder to give away?
— To whom could we give each of these items? Who needs them most? Who would enjoy them the most?
— What do you think it will mean to the person who gets this item? What will it mean to *you* to give away this item? What do you think it means to *God* that you're giving this item?

Together deliver the items you've decided to give away.

Music ᐯᐯᐯᐯᐯᐯᐯᐯᐯᐯᐯᐯᐯ

If your family sings together, learn and enjoy the song "Friends with God," found on page 24. Remember that the four verses of the song correspond to the four sessions of *Growing a Grateful, Generous Heart*; we will refer to this song again in Session 4. This week, review the first two verses and the chorus, then together learn the third verse.

Music Option

☐ *New Verses*

Try writing new verses for "Friends with God." Change the first two lines of the third verse to reflect ways in which individual family members give to God and others, for example:

And God loves Juanita,
Who makes her family laugh.
She is a friend of Jesus,
And that makes Jesus glad.

or

And God loves Jake and Jesse,
Who share their gift of song.
They are both friends of Jesus,
And that makes Jesus glad.

Praying Together ᐯᐯᐯᐯᐯᐯᐯ

There are as many ways to pray as there are people who pray. Each week we'll suggest a few ideas to choose from, or use those from other sessions. You can also combine prayer methods.

Prayer Options

☐ *Sentence-Completion Prayer*

Take turns completing one or more of the following incomplete prayers:

— Dear God, thank you for the gift of...
— Caring God, if I could share one of the gifts you've given me, it would be...
— Generous God, help me to share my...
— Giving God, one gift I like to give is...
— Loving God, a way I could share your love with someone this week is...
— Jesus, if you could say something to the widow, I think it would be...
— Jesus, if you could say one thing to me about giving, I think it might be...

☐ *Little Gifts*

Stand together in a circle. Ask:

— What little gifts could we give each other right now?

If family members need help, suggest any or all of the following: *a hug, a kiss, the words "I love you", the words "I'm glad you're my sister," holding a hand, a smile, a tender touch, an arm around a shoulder*, etc. Give these gifts to one another, then close by saying, in unison:

— Thank you, God, for little gifts. *Amen.*

☐ *Prayer Book*
From *The Book of Common Prayer*, pray either of the Prayers "For Guidance" (#57 or #58, p. 832), replacing the italicized *thy* and *thee* with *your* and *you*. To make the prayer even more understandable and personal, invite family members to rewrite the prayer in their own words, perhaps doing a phrase or two each day. Write the prayer on a large sheet of light-colored construction paper or a piece of poster board, and the readers in your family will be able to pray the prayer in unison.

☐ *Prayer Song*
Sing the song "Friends with God," found in Session 1 on page 24. Or sing "Take my life, that I may be," #707 in *The Hymnal 1982*.

☐ *Stewardship Prayer*
Learn and pray the Stewardship Prayer, found earlier in this session on page 39.

Chapter 4, Session 3: The Widow's Offering

Jesus Calls His Disciples

Part One: FOR PARENTS

Scripture

Luke 5:1-11

Theme

God's love and generosity may mean that we live differently than others.

Objectives

- to hear and respond to the call to follow Jesus
- to explore the practical implications of following Jesus
- to see faithful stewardship as a way of life

Activities

- Story: Jesus Calls His Disciples
- Checking In
- Giving Box
- Stewardship Prayer
- Art Response
- Second Story: The Story of Paul
- Around the Table
- Field Trip
- Music
- Praying Together

Scripture Summary

While ministering to people on the shore of Lake Gennesaret, Jesus asks Simon Peter to let him stand in his boat a little offshore, to better address the crowd. When finished speaking, Jesus instructs Peter and his co-workers to put down their nets in deeper water, resulting in a large catch of fish. Amazed, Peter, James and John respond to Jesus' invitation to join him. They become his first disciples.

Scripture Background

This reading offers Luke's version of the call of the first disciples. Although focused on Peter, it is more than just his story, for it illustrates the experience that every Christian disciple must undergo to follow Jesus. Peter's story is our story. His example reveals what following Christ will always require.

The call to discipleship begins with an everyday event that suddenly evokes wonder and a sense that there is "more" to what is going on than is immediately evident. After borrowing their boat for his teaching pulpit, Jesus rewards the fishermen, whose all-night toil had produced no results, with the promise of a fresh catch. Reluctantly the experienced fishermen go along with this carpenter's command.

The wondrous catch of fish is a sign that quickly prompts Peter to recognize that there is "more" to Jesus than his pleasing words. Peter realizes that this surprising catch is directly associated with God's power working through Jesus. Peter's awareness of God's presence in Jesus also makes him painfully aware of his wrong relationship

with God (sin) and eager to change his life. Peter assumes the position of a suppliant, asking Jesus to "Go away" yet holding on tightly to Jesus' knees.

Peter's experience of Jesus' generosity makes it impossible to be content with fishing. He wants to be with Jesus. But Jesus reveals that there are conditions for following him. First, "Don't be afraid" (v. 10). In the gospels, fear is the opposite of the basic trust that we identify as faith. Faith is the trust in another person that serves as the bond (Latin, *fides*) of a relationship. Because of that bond, we are willing to change our lives.

Second, Jesus indicates how Peter's life will change. Peter must redirect his life and reapply his previously-developed skills in service to Jesus' goal of establishing a kingdom community. Instead of luring fish into a net, Peter's new job will be "fishing" for people, bringing them into the net of Jesus' kingdom community.

Good stewardship requires a new way of seeing the world that allows us to recognize God's presence in our midst. It also demands a new way of being in the world so that we use our gifts and the skills that we have developed in order to create and build God's kingdom community of justice, love and peace in our world.

Reflection and Response

Ever so carefully, we dole out our time, treasure and talent. We weigh our tiny contributions as stingily as T. S. Eliot's J. Alfred Prufrock: "I have measured out my life with coffee spoons." Then a surprising outpouring of divine generosity tips the balance scales and we are astonished by the abundant grace. Even the things we rarely count are enormous blessings: waking each morning, enjoying fresh air and sunshine, having access to education, food and clean drinking water, medical care. Then if we start counting the people who intersect the paths of our lives, our opportunities for travel, service, friendship and work, our abilities to think, move, make music: the list is endless. Our paltry efforts to thank or repay God seem small by contrast.

Knowing that disparity may help us understand the scene by Lake Gennesaret. There, Peter and his coworkers move through an ordinary day, wash their nets and probably grumble about how few fish they've caught.

Suddenly, they confront stunning evidence of divine power. Most of us, from ill-fated attempts at fishing, know how hard it is to catch *one*. Imagine, then, our reaction to whole *nets* full, wet scales flashing silver in the sun, gills heaving and tails thrashing, weight straining against the nets, ropes threatening to rip. As two boats bulging with the catch sink dangerously close to the water line, we cast away our reasonable, plausible explanations. Our first instinct might be to gape, "Wow. Do that again." Then we might well say with Peter, "I'm out of my league here. Why not try the guys in the next boat?"

To Peter's credit, he instinctively recognizes the common root in the words "aw-ful" and "awe-some." His wonder, astonishment and humility are the beginnings of prayer and praise, but they are rare sentiments today. Sophisticated North Americans are a tough audience to impress. (We probably would've asked Jesus to toss in some

lobster, shrimp and—so it wouldn't seem fishy—filet mignon.)

Like Jesus' other miracles, this one has multiple layers of meaning. Just as physical healing connoted spiritual healing, so this multiplication is indicative of the apostles' ministry that would follow. To transpose Jesus' witticism about catching people into the current jargon, "you ain't seen nothing yet."

In beautiful symmetry, the abundant catch occurs both at the beginning and the end. Once again (John 21:1-14), Peter would be stupefied by a tremendous catch after the Resurrection. He is embarrassingly like ourselves: sometimes we "get it" only after the second, third or twenty-seventh repetition. Grace continues to pour into our lives: do we pay attention?

Was it then the flash and dazzle of the miracle that motivated the apostles, or the promise of personal changes to come? While our answers to that question may be speculative, it is more important to consider how we would answer it in our own lives. Do we understand how much is gift? In the end, will we be known for what we have achieved, or what we have been given? Which will we value more: success—or gratitude?

Read through the scripture passage. Quietly consider:
■ Name the blessings for which you are most grateful. If it is helpful, imagine them cascading forth like fish from a bulging net.

_____

_____

_____

_____

_____

_____

_____

_____

_____

My Own Story

My Calling

- How was the concept of "calling" addressed in your home? To what extent were you aware of your parents sense of "calling" or discipleship?

- At what age were you first aware of Jesus' invitation to follow and serve him? What did you believe that would involve? Was that scary? exciting? challenging? motivating?

- Once you understood that being a Christian also meant modeling the life of Jesus (helping and serving others; sharing the good news of God's love), what was your response? How throughout your life have you answered that call?

- How have you come to understand the nature of your call? If someone asked, "To what is Jesus calling you today?" how would you answer? How, in practical terms, do you do that?

_____

_____

_____

_____

_____

_____

_____

_____

_____

Being Counter-Cultural

- In your faith journey, at what points have you been aware of the "counter-cultural" nature of Christian faith? Where do you find faith and culture to be in conflict?

- How do you handle the pressure of consumerism? To what extent have you found the balance between consumption and responsible stewardship? In this process, what has been helpful? What has hindered your progress?

- What messages do you send your children in the way in which you handle money? acquire things? share your goods? How have you seen your values reflected in the behavior of your children?

- How do you apply faith disciplines in your use of time and talent, such as keeping Sabbath, seeing yourself as a collection of gifts from God, and discerning ways to use those gifts to God's purpose?

_____

_____

_____

_____

_____

_____

_____

_____

_____

Chapter 4, Session 4: Jesus Calls His Disciples

Story: Jesus Calls His Disciples

Soon after your child hears the story of Jesus' calling Peter, James and John in the session at church, review the story together, perhaps at the conclusion of a meal or just before bedtime. Children appreciate repetition, so don't hesitate to repeat the story several times, perhaps choosing several different approaches throughout the week.

Story Options

☐ *Child's Storytelling*
Invite your child to tell you the story of the miraculous catch of fish as he or she recalls it from the week's session at church.

☐ *Children's Paper*
Look together at the Children's Paper that your child brought home from the session at Church. Children in grades 1-2 could read the story to the family, perhaps at the conclusion of a meal together. Children in grades 3-6 could read the story directly from the Bible.

☐ *Children's Bible*
Read together the story of Jesus' calling Peter, James and John from a children's Bible or Bible storybook, for example:
— *Row the Boat: Jesus Fills the Nets* by Mary Manz Simon (St. Louis, MO: Concordia, 1990)

☐ *Act It Out*
Invite all family members to participate in acting out the story. To start, read the story aloud from the Bible, a children's Bible or a Bible storybook. Then assign the roles of *Jesus, Peter, James* and *John*. Add other characters if you like, for example, *the crowd, the boat, the net* or even *the fish!* Encourage creativity, improvise props and let all players create their own dialogue. You can encourage family members in their roles by asking such questions as:
— Jesus, what were you saying to the people on the shore? Why did you tell the fishermen to fish in deeper water? Did you really expect them to follow you when you invited them?
— Peter, James and John, what was your first thought when Jesus told you to go fishing again? What did you say when you saw the nets filled with fish? What do you think it means to "catch people"?

Checking In

Discover what your child *really* thinks about following Jesus. Here are several activities to help children express themselves. Remember, no matter what responses you might get—even ones that surprise you—affirm all answers, respect your child's feelings and opinions, and occasionally restate what your child says to make sure you've understood.

Check-In Options

☐ *Follow the Leader*
Invite family members to play a game of Follow the Leader. Connect the game to today's story by including actions drawn from the story, for example, rowing a boat, speaking to people, tossing a net, swimming like a fish. Give every family member a chance to be *Leader*. After the game, discuss:
— What do you like better, being the *Leader* or being a *Follower?*
— When at school (home, with family, with friends, at work) are you a leader? a follower?
— When would you rather be a leader? When would you rather be a follower?

☐ *Family Talk—What It Means to Follow*
Explore with family members the ways in which they follow and are followed:
— What does it mean to follow someone? *(Define this broadly; include people who lead at home, church, work, school, etc., as well as people who serve as models for family members.)*

Chapter 4, Session 4: Jesus Calls His Disciples

— Whom do you follow? Why do you follow these people? What kind of person would you follow? What kind of person would you *not* follow?
— Who follows *you?* Why do they follow you?
— What makes someone a good leader? What makes *you* a good leader?
— What kind of leader is Jesus? Why do you think the disciples in this week's story were so willing to follow Jesus?

Giving Box 〰〰〰〰〰〰

For a complete description of the Giving Box, along with suggestions for its use, see Session 1, page 21, Session 2, pages 30-31 and Session 3, page 39. Below are two additional suggestions:

Giving Box Options

☐ *Family Talk—Our Gift Box and the Call of Jesus*
Explore the close tie between your Giving Box and today's story. You might discuss:
— In what ways is our Giving Box like the net the disciples threw into the lake?
— Imagine that Jesus is sitting with us at the table. He looks around and says, "I think it would be a great idea if you used the money in your Giving Box to..." What might he say?

☐ *Donating Our Gifts*
Have you decided yet what to do with the money in your Giving Box? If not, together decide who will receive your gift and when, as a family, you will make this donation. Remember, a hands-on experience will make the gift all the more meaningful for both the recipient and the givers.

Stewardship Prayer 〰〰〰〰

In the sessions at church, some children are learning this prayer, repeating it every week at the conclusion of their session. You could also use the prayer at home throughout the four weeks of *Growing a Grateful, Generous Heart.* See the *Options* following the prayer.

Prayer

Thank you, Jesus, for bringing us together in your love.
Thank you for giving us everything we need.
Help us to take good care of the gifts you've given us.
Help us to use them to do your work. *Amen.*

Stewardship Prayer Options

☐ *Prayer Poster*
If you created the Prayer Poster in Session 1 (p. 21), use it as you continue to pray the Stewardship Prayer.

☐ *Prayer Booklet*
If you began the Prayer Booklet project in Session 1 (p. 22), finish it this week. Consider with whom you might share your completed booklet, perhaps family friends? a neighbor? a grandparent?

☐ *Discussion*
As a family, explore more of the prayer's meaning. You could ask:
— In our Stewardship Prayer we say to God, "Help us to use [the gifts you give us] to do your work."
— What "work" of God might be uniquely ours? *(If necessary, be more specific, for example, "What work of God could we do with our allowance money? with our time with friends? How could we help others with our toys and games? with our ability to run? to jump? to tell jokes?)*
— How can we "take good care" of the things God has given us? *(for example, bikes, brothers and sisters, good health, forests and rivers)*

☐ *Praying with Movement*
Invite family members to make up movements for each line of the prayer. Do the movements together as you pray the prayer. Movements will make the prayer easier to remember.

Art Response 〰〰〰〰〰〰

Complete one or more of the art projects suggested below. Remember, the goal is not the final product, but the time spent together exploring the Bible story and learning about each other.

Art Options

☐ *Uniquely Me*

For each family member, cut out a large, simple silhouette from poster board; see the illustration below. (If you have access to continuous newsprint or butcher paper, you could trace around each family member to create life-size silhouettes.) Tape or tack these to a wall at an easy-to-reach level for each family member. Invite everyone to use felt markers to add details to their silhouettes so that each silhouette uniquely represents that person, for example, 7-year-old Joanna could write her name, draw her favorite sweater, and add small pictures of her cat, a jump-rope and a book, representing three things she really enjoys.

Starting now, and continuing throughout the week, encourage family members to add words or drawings to their silhouettes that identify more of the things they can do and the things in which they are interested—that is, all the things that make them uniquely who they are, all the things they might be able to share with others. If everyone agrees, they

Second Story: The Story of Paul

Especially for older children, it can be challenging and revealing to link scripture stories with similar themes. This week, if you wish, explore several events in the life of the Apostle Paul, who, like Peter, John and James in today's story, had a remarkable, direct call to follow Jesus. We suggest reading at least the story of Paul's conversion (listed first), then one or two other stories from Paul's life, either directly from the Bible, a children's Bible or a Bible storybook:

■ Acts 9:1-19 (the story of Paul's conversion)
■ Acts 14:8-18 (Paul and Barnabas mistaken for gods)
■ Acts 16:16-34 (the conversion of the Philippian jailer)
■ Acts 19:11-20 (the man with the evil spirit)
■ Acts 27:13-44 (the storm and shipwreck at sea)

If you wish, discuss:

■ How did Jesus call Paul (then called Saul)?
■ What different experiences did Paul have as he followed after Jesus? What dangers did he face? How did God keep him safe through all these dangers?
■ Paul preached wherever he went, even when it was dangerous. What was Paul's message?
■ Imagine you are traveling with Paul. What is scary about being with him? What is exciting?
■ Imagine that we could invite both Peter and Paul over for dinner. What would you like to talk about with them? What would you like to ask them? to tell them?

Feel free to adapt any other activity from these sessions to explore the story further (like acting out the story or sculpting scenes from it).

could also add to each others' silhouettes what they see as their abilities and interests. Take time during the week to review additions to the silhouettes, acknowledging and affirming everyone's unique mix of abilities and interests.

At some point you could discuss:
— You are unique. In all the world, there is only one you. Why do you think God gave you your special mix of interests and abilities?
— Jesus invites us to follow him, to use our gifts and interests to help others. Choose any three of the words or pictures on your silhouette. How might you use each of these to help others? to spread the good news of God's love?

☐ *Tithing Circle*
To start, review the section on Tithing in Chapter 2 (p. 11). If you think it's appropriate, share this information with family members. Then, in this activity, help family members understand the concept of the tithe by creating a "Tithing Circle."

Cut a big circle out of a large sheet of poster board. Using a felt marker, divide the circle into 10 roughly equal wedges (like a pie). Now cut 10 wedge-shaped pieces out of colored construction paper, made to fit the sections of the circle. Make each wedge a different color.

Together with family members, draw illustrations on each construction-paper wedge:
— On each of nine of the 10 wedges, draw a picture of something on which your family regularly (weekly or monthly) spends money, for example, food, clothes, electricity, recreation, books, movie tickets, video rentals, medical care, hobbies, etc. Talk together about what each drawing ought to be, and help family members (especially younger children) understand that there are costs associated with each of them. You could estimate dollar amounts for these items and write the amounts on the wedges. As you complete each wedge, tape it to a section of the circle.
— Before drawing or writing on the tenth wedge, discuss: "Some people believe that God asks them to give one-tenth of their money back to

God." Count the 10 sections of the circle. Point out that in nine of the 10 you have written/drawn items that you buy for your family. Now, invite family members to suggest what to write or draw on the tenth wedge: "In what ways could we *(or do we)* use some of our money (one-tenth) to give back to God? to help others? to support our church?" Together decide what to put on the 10th wedge; include several suggestions. After you've completed this last wedge, tape it to the final section of the circle.

Draw or write a number of ideas on this tenth wedge, including ways in which *all* family members, no matter their age, can "give back to God." Obviously, wage-earners can contribute money, both to the church and to other causes, but everyone in the family can give in some way, through time spent volunteering, sharing their gifts and interests with others, etc.

☐ *"Fish" Gift Certificates*
If you did not choose to use the "Coin" Gift Certificates described in Session 3 (p. 42), do this variation, which uses "fish" instead of "coins" as "gift certificates" to distribute to friends, neighbors or each other. First invite every family member to think of several ways in which they could give to (or help) someone else, for example:
— baby-sitting for an evening
— raking a lawn
— cooking a meal
— playing a game
— going for a walk
— sharing a favorite toy
— doing a chore
— giving a 10-minute shoulder rub

Each of these gifts will be written on a fish-shaped "gift certificate" to be redeemed by the recipient. Fish could be cut from cardboard or colored construction paper. On each fish, family members write out one "gift" they are willing to give someone. Possible text for the certificates could be:
— Entitles the bearer to play a game of their choice with me. Redeemable anytime.
— Good for 3 hours of baby-sitting by Janice. Just say when!

Chapter 4, Session 4: Jesus Calls His Disciples

You could decorate the coins with additional designs: eyes, scales, mouths, etc. Consider adding the reference for today's story of Jesus' calling of his disciples, Luke 5:1-11.

When finished, encourage family members to hand deliver their completed fish, and, of course, to follow through on their gifts.

Around the Table ᐧᐧᐧᐧᐧ

Family mealtimes, either at home or out, can be a great place to explore the themes of *Growing a Grateful, Generous Heart.*

Table Options

☐ *Family Talk—Listening Game*
A big part of following is listening. Play this listening game before discussing when, how and why we listen, both to each other, and to God. Explain to family members that you will give a simple suggestion, and if they can hear you, they can do the action you suggest. Each time you offer a suggestion, change the level of your voice, sometimes speaking softly, sometimes loudly. At times speak so softly that you can't be heard. We offer a few suggestions here, but add many more of your own:
— If you can hear my voice, touch your nose.
— If you can hear my voice, laugh out loud.
— If you can hear my voice, scratch your ear.

Invite other family members to offer suggestions as well. After playing, discuss:
— Who have you listened to today?
— When have you missed out on something because you didn't listen?
— When is it really important to listen?
— When is listening hard? easy?
— How do we listen to God?
— How could we listen to God right now? *(hearing a Bible story, being silent, listening to each other, etc.)*

☐ *Family Affirmations*
Sometimes what is obvious to others is hard to see in ourselves, including the ways in which we follow and serve Jesus in our daily lives. In this activity, family members identify ways in which they see God at work in and through each other. You could do this as simply as inviting family members to complete this statement for every other person at the table:
— *(Name), you follow Jesus when you...*

☐ *Family Talk—Instead of Buying New...*
Pick an item that you or someone in your family has been considering buying, for example, a lawn mower, a tape player or piece of furniture. Together consider each of these alternatives, in the following order:
— Do we really need this item, or could we get along without it?
— If we really need it, is there a similar item we already own that could be used? Is there one we could clean up or restore?
— If we own nothing similar, is it something we could borrow temporarily from a friend or neighbor?
— If no one can loan this item to us, would a friend, neighbor or community group like to co-own it with us, cutting our cost and saving resources (not to mention creating community)?
— If we do need to buy it, how can we do so most responsibly? For example, will a used tape player purchased at a garage sale, secondhand store or online auction site play tapes as well as a new one from the mall?
— When we select this item, can we find one that is environmentally friendly and recyclable when we are through with it?

Repeat the exercise for several other items.

Field Trip 〜〜〜〜〜〜〜〜〜

Following Jesus often means making counter-cultural choices, saying "no" to the messages that bombard us whenever we walk through a store, drive down the street, retrieve the mail, go on-line, watch TV, listen to the radio or read a magazine. Even our pantry shelves are filled with advertising—the labels found on every product. The outings suggested below help you, as a family, take steps to counter this barrage of consumer influence.

Field Trip Options

☐ *The Mall Game*
With older children, take a stroll through a nearby mall, making a game of identifying the many ways in which retailers manipulate us into spending money. You can start by pointing out several examples yourself, as we list here:
— Look for advertising in unusual places, for example, on shopping carts, in the floor or on displays in hallways.
— Note the behavior of sales people, for example, clerks' standing in aisles offering samples of cologne or cosmetics.
— Observe store displays. What kinds of items are placed where, and why? What do they do with color? lighting? other props or photographs? What feeling are they trying to create? What do they do differently for adults? teens? kids?
— Ask: "If you were trying to hook someone your age into buying something, even if they didn't need it, what would you do?" Now look for examples of these approaches in the mall.
— Challenge the messages you see in store displays. For example, are all the manikins and models in the photographs slim, young and sexy? How realistic is that? how does that sell products?

☐ *Visit a Recycling Center*
Look in the phone book or online for a recycling center near your home. Call and see if you can visit; most will be happy to show what they do and provide additional information. Learn about the process of recycling and how your family can participate.

☐ *Second-Hand Trip*
Gather clothes, housewares and other donatable items in good condition. As a family, take them to your local Goodwill, ARC or other secondhand store. Donate the items, but then spend some time in the store shopping for items your family needs. Help family members understand:
— Even if your family hasn't needed to shop at a secondhand store, many families do.
— We conserve valuable resources by recycling clothes and other household items.
— Profits from many secondhand stores (like both Goodwill and ARC) help to fund programs for the needy and physically challenged.
— Our family saves money when we buy recycled items. We can use that money for other things, including sharing with those in need.

☐ *Web Tour*
Gather around the family computer for a virtual field trip. Below we list several Websites. At these sites you'll find suggestions for individuals and families looking to simplify their lives and live more responsibly in relationship to others, God and the earth. As a family, explore one or more of these sites. Print out helpful information. Discuss what you find:
— The PBS show *Affluenza* has an excellent Website, including resources geared for kids and families: *www.pbs.org/kcts/affluenza*
— The Center for a New American Dream offers a downloadable booklet for parents titled *Tips for Parents in a Commercial Culture*, along with lots of other solid information: *www.newdream.org*
— Earth Ministry, a Seattle-based organization working "to connect Christian faith with care and justice for all creation," offers resources and information: *www.earthministry.com*
— Visit the Website of the Episcopal Church and check out what's happening at the Environmental Stewardship Office (*www.episcopalchurch.org/peace-justice/envstewardship.asp*), at UTO (*www.episcopalchurch.org/uto*), and at Episcopal Relief and Development (*www.er-d.org*).
— Explore the Episcopal Stewardship Office site and click on its links for and about children: (*www.episcopalchurch.org/congdev/Stewardship/Steward.htm*).

Chapter 4, Session 4: Jesus Calls His Disciples

Music

If your family sings together, learn and enjoy the song "Friends with God," found on page 24. Remember that the four verses of the song correspond to the four sessions of *Growing a Grateful, Generous Heart*. This week, review the first three verses and the chorus, then together learn the fourth verse.

Praying Together

There are as many ways to pray as there are people who pray. Each week we'll suggest a few ideas to choose from, or you may wish to use those from other sessions. You can also combine prayer methods.

Prayer Options

☐ *Roll-a-Prayer*

Borrow a die from a family game. Family members take turns rolling the die and offering simple prayers, based on this chart:

 Thank God for something you enjoy owning.

 Thank God for someone you enjoy knowing.

 Thank God for something you are glad you can do (a gift or talent).

 Tell God something nice you'd like to do for someone else.

 Ask God to help you do something.

 Ask God any question.

Alternative

Invite family members to assign the prayer elements for each side of the die.

☐ *Prayer Book*

From *The Book of Common Prayer*, pray "A Prayer of Self-Dedication" (#61, p. 832), replacing the italicized *thee, thine, thou* and *thy* with their contemporary counterparts. To make the prayer even more meaningful, discuss:

— How do you think God draws our hearts to God? How does God guide our minds? fill our imaginations? control our wills?

— If we were "utterly dedicated" to God, what would that look like? How would we treat others? ourselves? How would we talk?

Or pray "A Prayer Attributed to St. Francis" (#62, p. 833).

☐ *Prayer Song*

Sing the song "Friends with God," found in Session 1 on page 24. Or sing "O Jesus, I have promised," #655 in *The Hymnal 1982*.

☐ *Stewardship Prayer*

Learn and pray the Stewardship Prayer, found earlier in this session on page 49.

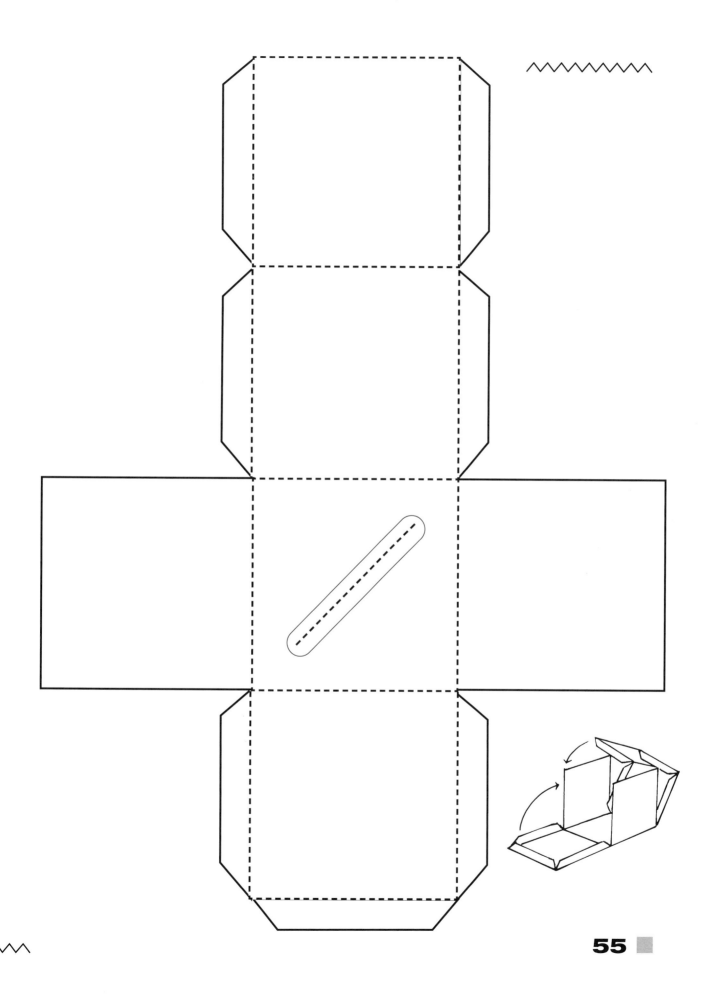